The Legacies of Caribbean Radical Politics

The year 2009 marked the 50th anniversary of the Cuban Revolution and the thirtieth anniversary of the Grenadian and Nicaraguan Revolutions, and as such offered an occasion to assess the complex legacies of revolutionary politics in the Caribbean. This volume considers what we might learn from such revolutionary projects and their afterlives, from their successes and their errors. It explores what struggles, currently underway in the Caribbean, share with these earlier and longer revolutionary traditions, and how they depart from them. It analyzes radical movements in Jamaica, Grenada, Cuba, Venezuela, Guadeloupe, Suriname, and Guyana, not only in their national dimensions, but in terms of their regional linkages and mutual influences.

The chapters are drawn from various disciplines and a range of democratic leftist projects. They consider not only state and party politics, but also civil society, cultural politics and artistic production, strikes, and grassroots activism.

This book was published as a special issue of *Interventions: International Journal of Postcolonial Studies*.

Shalini Puri is an Associate Professor of English at the Univerisity of Pittsburgh. She is the author of *The Caribbean Postcolonial: Social Equality, Post-Nationalism, and Cultural Hybridity* (Palgrave Macmillan 2004), which won the Gordon and Sybil Lewis Award for best book about the Caribbean, and has edited *Marginal Migrations: The Circulation of Cultures within the Caribbean* (2003). She is currently completing a book entitled *Volcanic Memory: The Grenada Revolution and the Futures of Revolutionary Practice*. She is also working on a collaborative project entitled 'Theorizing Fieldwork in the Humanities'.

The Legacies of Caribbean Radical Politics

Edited by Shalini Puri

Routledge
Taylor & Francis Group

LONDON AND NEW YORK

First published 2011
by Routledge
2 Park Square, Milton Park, Abingdon, Oxon, OX14 4RN

Simultaneously published in the USA and Canada
by Routledge
711 Third Avenue, New York, NY 10017

Routledge is an imprint of the Taylor & Francis Group, an informa business

© 2011 Taylor & Francis

First issued in paperback 2013

This book is a reproduction of *Interventions: International Journal of Postcolonial Studies,* vol. 12, issue 1. The Publisher requests to those authors who may be citing this book to state, also, the bibliographical details of the special issue on which the book was based

Typeset in Minion by Value Chain, India

British Library Cataloguing in Publication Data
A catalogue record for this book is available from the British Library

ISBN13: 978-0-415-58689-4 (hbk)
ISBN13: 978-0-415-85124-4 (pbk)

Disclaimer
The publisher would like to make readers aware that the chapters in this book are referred to as articles as they had been in the special issue. The publisher accepts responsibility for any inconsistencies that may have arisen in the course of preparing this volume for print.

Contents

Notes on Contributors

Anthony Bogues is Harmon Family Professor of Africana Studies at Brown University. His latest books are *Empire of Liberty: Power, Desire and Freedom* and *Caribbean Thought: The Literature and Politics of History.* He is currently a humanities faculty fellow at the Cogut Humanities Center, Brown University where he is writing a book titled, *And what about the Human? The Literatures and Politics of Freedom in Radical Anti-Colonial Thought.*

Yarimar Bonilla is an Assistant Professor of Anthropology at the University of Virginia. She is currently working on a book entitled, *A Striking Past: Labor and the Politics of History in the French Antilles.*

Merle Collins is a Grenadian writer, and a Professor of Comparative Literature and English at the University of Maryland, College Park. She served in Grenada's Ministry of Foreign Affairs during the Grenada Revolution. Her publications include the novels *Angel* and *The Colour of Forgetting*; a collection of short stories entitled *Rain Darling*; and several volumes of poetry, including *Rotten Pomerack* and *Lady in a Boat*, as well as several critical essays.

Raphael Dalleo is Assistant Professor of English at Florida Atlantic University. His articles have appeared in journals such as *Small Axe, ARIEL, South Asian Review*, and the *Journal of West Indian Literature.* He is coauthor of *The Latino/a Canon and the Emergence of Post-Sixties Literature* (Palgrave Macmillan, 2007), and is currently completing a manuscript called *Caribbean Literature and the Public Sphere: From Anticolonial to Postcolonial.*

Annalee Davis works as a multi-media visual artist in Barbados. Her video, "On the Map", explores the movement of people from Guyana into Barbados within the context of the CSME, questioning notions of home and belonging. The installation, "Just Beyond my Imagination", remaps the Caribbean as a golf course - a playground where islands become sand traps and the sea transforms into astro-turf. For more information, visit http://www.annaleedavis.com

Sujatha Fernandes is an Assistant Professor of Sociology at Queens College and the Graduate Center of the City University of New York. She is the author of *Cuba Represent! Cuban Arts, State Power, and the Making of New Revolutionary Cultures* (Duke University Press, October 2006). Her second book, *Who Can Stop the*

Drums? Urban Social Movements in Chávez's Venezuela is forthcoming with Duke University Press in Spring 2010.

Norman Girvan (http://normangirvan.info) is Professorial Research Fellow in the Institute of International Relations at the University of the West Indies (UWI) in Trinidad. He has been Secretary General of the Association of Caribbean States, Head of Economic Planning in the Government of Jamaica, and Director of the UWI's Sir Arthur Lewis Institute of Social and Economic Studies. He is the author of several books and numerous journal articles on the political economy of development in the Caribbean and the Global South.

Rafael Hernández is a political scientist, a researcher and the editor of *Temas*, an academic journal based in Havana. He has taught at universities in Cuba, the U.S., Mexico and Puerto Rico. His most recent books are *Looking at Cuba: Essays on Culture and Civil Society* (Critics National Award, 2001), *The Other War: Studies on Strategy and International Security* (2000), and *The History of Havana* (coauthored with D. Cluster, 2006).

Rafael Rojas is Professor and Researcher, Center for Economic Research and Teaching, Mexico City, and he has been Visiting Professor at Princeton and Columbia University. He has written or edited more than fifteen books on Cuban, Mexican and Latin American culture. His book, *Tumbas sin sosiego. Revolución, disidencia y exilio del intelectual cubano* (2006), received The Premio Anagrama, one of the most prestigious prizes for essays in the Hispanic world. His latest book is *El estante vacío. Literatura y política en Cuba* (Anagrama, 2009).

Shalini Puri is an Associate Professor of English at the University of Pittsburgh. She has written *The Caribbean Postcolonial: Social Equality, Post-Nationalism, and Cultural Hybridity* (2004), which won the Gordon and Sybil Lewis Award for best book on the Caribbean, and has edited *Marginal Migrations: The Circulation of Cultures within the Caribbean* (2003). In April 2009 at the University of Pittsburgh, she convened the conference "Remembering the Future: Radical Politics in the Caribbean," at which many of the essays in this volume were first presented. She is currently completing a book entitled *Volcanic Memory: The Grenada Revolution and the Futures of Revolutionary Practice*. She is also working on a collaborative project entitled *Theorizing Fieldwork in the Humanities*.

Rupert Roopnaraine holds a Ph.D in Comparative Literature from Cornell. He co-led the Working People's Alliance in Guyana with Walter Rodney until Rodney's assassination; he has also served as an MP in Guyana. He remains in the leadership of the WPA. His publications include *The Primacy of the Eye: The Art of Stanley Greaves* (2004); *The Web of October: Rereading Martin Carter* (1988); a volume of poetry entitled *Suite for Supriya* (1991), and *In the Sky's Wild Noise:*

Selected Essays (forthcoming from Peepal Tree Press, 2010). He has also written and directed a film on political memory entitled *The Terror and the Time* (1977), a prize winning documentary on the environment, *The SeaWall – Tales from the Guyana Coast* (1991), and *The Visual Imagination in the Caribbean* (1993).

Kathy Sloane has been making photographs in the Caribbean, jazz clubs, and the San Francisco Bay Area for 35 years. In 1983 she lived in Grenada and photographed for UNICEF and the Grenadian Government. Her documentary film "Witness to Hiroshima" was released in 2008.

Alissa Trotz is Associate Professor of Women and Gender Studies, and Director of Caribbean Studies, University of Toronto. Her essays have appeared in *Social and Economic Studies*, *Small Axe*, *New West Indian Guide*, *Caribbean Review of Gender Studies*, and *Global Networks*. She co-edited (with Aaron Kamugisha) a special issue of *Race and Class* (Volume 49, 2007) commemorating the 200th anniversary of the abolition of the British slave trade. She edits a weekly column, "In the Diaspora," in the Guyanese daily *The Stabroek News*, and is a member of Red Thread Women's Development Organization.

LEGACIES LEFT

The year 2009 marked the 50th anniversary of the Cuban Revolution and the 30th anniversary of the Grenadian and Nicaraguan Revolutions, and as such offered an occasion to assess the complex legacies of revolutionary politics in the Caribbean. This collection seeks to honor the aspirations and accomplishments of these very different Caribbean revolutions. It considers what we might learn from such revolutionary projects and their afterlives, from their successes and their errors. And it remembers sister struggles across the region that were also undertaken against enormous odds.

David Scott has asked: how do we need to modify or translate the great modern theorists of revolution to speak to the considerably changed political landscape we inhabit today? (Scott 2004). This volume explores Scott's question as a matter not only of theory but also of practice, turning to particular examples of ongoing radical political praxis in the Caribbean as sites where such modifications and translations are taking place. Thus we ask: To what extent have the very different revolutionary processes of Cuba, Grenada, and Nicaragua, shaped the ground or horizon of possibility of subsequent movements in the region? What do struggles currently underway in the Caribbean share with these earlier and longer revolutionary traditions, and how do they depart from them? What forms of political organization, what kinds of alliances and fractures have emerged in different periods in the Caribbean, and what are their implications?

In a kind of eulogy to the armed struggles of Latin America in the 1970s and the 1980s, John Beverley both recognizes them as belonging to a moment past and refutes demonizing representations of them. 'A more comprehensive rethinking of the armed struggle would have to involve a critique of the misconceptions, arrogance, and just plain foolishness often involved in both its theory and practice. Even so, the promise of the armed struggle pointed to the possibility of a more egalitarian and joyful future. It did not fail because of its internal contradictions – although there were many – nor was it condemned to defeat from the start; it was defeated by what turned out to be in the end a stronger, more ruthless enemy' (Beverly 2009: 58).

This volume participates in a related debate over memory, attending to the *mixed* legacies of radical politics. We remember here some of the best examples of democratic socialist practice that the region created, the forms of participatory democracy it developed. These include, for example, the zonal councils and open popular assemblies in Grenada and Nicaragua. They include also the Sandinistas' move – not once they had consolidated the revolution, but in 1979, the very year the Revolution came to power – to abolish the death penalty. In fact, the massive electoral participation that continued even in the years after the defeat of the Sandinista Revolution reflects the latter's legacy of popular political mobilization. Cuba's Family Code and Maternity Laws of the mid-1970s and similar legislation in Grenada and Nicaragua initiated a project of transforming relations of gender inequity, a project which subsequent feminisms drew on, revised, and extended. Cuba delivered, free and to its entire people, some of the highest quality healthcare in the world, reducing infant mortality and raising life expectancy for its people. Its doctors trained doctors around the global south. And as we rightly remember the forms of political and cultural censorship that these revolutions enacted, we should also remember the ways in which they brought the arts to working people and working people to the arts.

If, like Beverley, this collection acknowledges the unrelenting military, economic, and cultural aggressions of neo-colonialism and imperialism, and the authoritarian violence of Right wing regimes in the region, such aggressions are the ground of this collection rather than its focus. These continual forms of violence have exerted immense pressure on Left politics in the region – both in terms of the resources that the Left has had to divert towards defense, and in terms of the Left's treatment of dissent. One question that animates this collection, therefore, is precisely how to avoid such aggressions being turned into alibis for Left authoritarianism and how, *given* imperial and right wing aggression, the Left can deepen its democratic practices. As the Cuban film director Tomás Guitierrez Alea once remarked in conversation, 'Socialism is a great script, but with poor directors' (Chanan 2004: 8).

Importantly, then, the collection also remembers and identifies particular errors, failures and miscalculations of revolutionary projects in the region – not as part of a narrative of disillusionment, betrayal, or rejection of the Left, nor as part of a complacent narrative of its inevitable transcendence, but as part of a project to renew and strengthen the promise of the Left. These are not abstract questions. They are both ethical and strategic. Twenty six years ago, the Grenada Revolution fell because it could not find a way to put the answers into practice. The combination of a tiny, tightly-run paternalistic vanguard party, the imprisoning of dissidents, the practice not only of necessary self defense, but of an *ethos* of militarism and military solutions: all these brought down the Revolution's highest aspirations, resulting in fratricide and a setback to egalitarian mass politics in the region in ways from which the latter is still recovering. The Cuban Revolution has a much longer, more complex, and shifting history of suppressing, permitting, and managing disagreement within the Left, as the essays in this collection show. The object of this effort, then, is not an abstract auto-critique of the Left, but a more focused recall of particular instances, one that identifies the strategic alternatives that were available or might now be so. This volume is thus conceived as a debate not between Left and Right, but as an open dialogue between different Left formations and projects.

Finally, integral to the essays in this collection is an analysis of Left struggles in the region not only in terms of the particular nations in which they were centered, but in terms of their regional linkages. It is worth remembering, then, that in 1767, Henri Christophe of the Haitian Revolution was born on the Sans Souci estate of Grenada, from where he was taken to Haiti as a slave. That Fedon, who led the Fedon's Rebellion in 1795 in Grenada, inspired by the same events that inspired the Haitian Revolution, evaded the British military, and according to popular memory is said to have escaped to Cuba. Or that early meetings towards a 'One Caribbean Revolution' took place in 1970 in St Lucia or that Grenada's New Jewel Movement held one of its first meetings in Martinique in 1972. Or that the US invasion of Grenada was rehearsed in Vieques, Puerto Rico. And that the fall of the Grenada Revolution shaped Suriname's rightward turn, and probably played a part in Nicaragua's moving to hold elections in 1984.

Many of the essays collected here demonstrate what I think of as the tangled intimacy of Caribbean relations. 'The unity is submarine,' said Kamau Brathwaite about the Caribbean, a statement that finds its motivation in what it leaves implicit: that unity is far from apparent much of the time (Brathwaite 1974). Or as Paul Keens-Douglas put it with skeptical and stinging humor:

'Tell me again /
bout de big island
an de small island,
bout de rich island
an de poor island,
how all ah we is one,
an how Cari-come
an Cari-gone,
tell me again' (Keens-Douglas 1986: 56).

The Caribbean is a region imagined, constituted, and maintained through the historical experiences of colonization, slavery and indentureship, trans-Atlantic and intra-Caribbean migrations, various articulations of global capitalism and neoliberal trade arrangements (NAFTA, CARICOM, the Caribbean Single Market Economy, the Economic Partnership Agreement), the short-lived reality of Federation, transnational and grassroots organizing, and ALBA (the Alianza Bolivariana para los Pueblos de Nuestra América). This volume begins a consideration of how various Left movements have intervened in and contributed to these many competing regionalisms of the Caribbean. What forms of internationalism, what regional links and alliances, are now being forged, not only at the state level, but also at the grassroots and familial levels? What does 'Cuba' or 'Haiti' mean in the popular memory of the Caribbean? What does 'Grenada' evoke in Cuban popular and official memory? What links have been made or are possible between different youth cultures across the Caribbean? How have Left organizational strategies necessarily been different in the sovereign or nominally sovereign, and the non-sovereign Caribbean? What are the emerging relations between the Caribbean and the surging Left movements of Latin America?

While these questions have defined this project, the collection does not by any means answer them all. Nor does it take up more than a few instances of radical practice from the Caribbean. The campaign in Vieques, Puerto Rico spearheaded by independentistas and transformed into a mass popular movement which successfully closed down the US military base there in 2003; the Peace Management Initiative in Jamaica; post-Aristide efforts at organizing in Haiti; multi-racial women's movements in Trinidad, Guyana, and elsewhere, that have increasingly asserted their autonomy from being merely wings of political parties; Feministas in Resistencia who have continually confronted and opposed the anti-Zelaya coup in Honduras earlier in 2009; peasant alliances in Haiti which in 2008 and 2009 agitated for an end to the food crisis; successful indigenous organizing for land rights in Suriname; the fair trade and banking initiatives of ALBA; innumerable local grassroots groups across the Caribbean that daily work towards the enfranchisement and equality of Caribbean people, intervening variously in civil society, the state, and the global market: all these are absent from this issue, yet inform it. Part of the hope of this volume is simply to evoke the density with which the landscape of political radicalism in the Caribbean is plotted, and to suggest some terms for discussing it. Equally, the relevance of the analyses and histories recounted here is not confined to the immediate sites they address, but extends across the Caribbean and beyond to the global south.

The collection is organized into two roughly equal halves: the first treats Cuba and Grenada; the second treats particular instances of left mobilization elsewhere in the region, spanning 1938 to the present.

It opens with the remarkable essay 'Resonances of Revolution' by Rupert Roopnaraine, which captures the events of the Grenada Revolution – from the heady sense of possibility of its beginnings to its devastating fall – as they spilled over into neighboring Guyana and Suriname. He evokes the shifting terrain, the press and rush of overlapping Left mobilizations in the region at the time, the suspense and anticipation as to their outcomes, and the specific efforts of the Working People's Alliance, which Roopnaraine co-led with Walter Rodney, to elaborate a Marxism independent of Moscow. The essay is significant for several reasons: It has a substantial discussion of Suriname, a country which is too often marginalized in Caribbean Studies. It illuminates the intricacy and delicacy of intra-Left negotiations and alliances in the region. And it breaks a twenty-six year silence: Here for the first time, Roopnaraine publicly comments on his efforts at mediating the October 1983 crisis in Grenada.

In some ways a mirror-image of this essay, Merle Collins's 'Are you a Bolshevik or a Menshevik?' begins with traumatic fall of the Grenada Revolution. Its tone is strikingly and movingly different from that of Roopnaraine's, powerfully evoking the intense solitude in which its struggle to understand and rethink the same events took place. Collins focuses on the relationship of the Grenada Revolution with Black Power, Marxism-Leninism, and anti-imperialism. If Roopnaraine's essay traces the pan-Caribbean consequences of the Grenada Revolution, Collins compares the (mis)fortunes of Leninism in Grenadian and Soviet histories. Moreover, she returns to Lenin's writings, and unlike the many accounts that attribute the fall of the Grenada Revolution to Leninism, Collins suggests that perhaps the problem arose from a mechanical and inadequate application of Leninism, coupled with the subordination of Grenadian experience to Soviet experience.

Rafael Hernández' essay, 'The Cuban Revolution and the Caribbean' is remarkable in that it studies not only Cuba's relatively well-documented assistance to numerous liberation struggles in the global south, but also because it reveals a reciprocity of influence: for example, how pan-Africanism and Grenada required a rethinking of Cuban Marxism by the state, and how the Caribbean Council of Churches helped make possible a shift in Cuba away from the atheism of Soviet Marxist orthodoxy. The portrait that emerges from Hernández's essay is of a Cuban state and a Cuban socialism that are dynamic, responsive, and flexible.

In contrast, Rafael Rojas in his trenchant essay 'The Content of Socialism in Cuba Today' rejects the feasibility of 'critical socialisms' such as those of Rafael Hernández and foreign neo-marxist theorists in solidarity with Cuba, who believe it is possible to work with(in) the Cuban state towards greater democratization of Cuban society. Rojas argues that as long as a single-party Cuban state is the final and only permitted arbiter of culture, no transformation of Cuban socialism is possible.

The first half of the volume closes with an essay by Raphael Dalleo that relates the revolutions of Cuba and Grenada. Dalleo looks at selected novels, poetry, and essays of Trinidadian-born socialist feminist Dionne Brand to investigate the place of Cuba in the wider Caribbean literary imagination. He traces in Brand's work the influence of the Cuban genres of *testimonio* and of narratives of collaboration between intellectuals and peasants. Unlike Rojas, Dalleo argues that, at least for Dionne Brand, the reasons for the shrinking horizon of revolutionary politics in the region lay not in events or errors in Cuba, but in Grenada. That is, Brand's work from 1984 to 1996 suggests to Dalleo that the Grenada Revolution is the point at which an anti-colonial revolutionary politics turns into a postcolonial poetics that mourns the loss of a revolutionary possibility which it continues to desire.

The second half of the volume begins with an essay that studies radical politics in the Caribbean prior to the Cuban Revolution, addressing the mass movements that shook the Caribbean in the 1930s, and questioning their designation as 'workers' rebellions'. Anthony Bogues addresses this period through the lens of the rebellions in Jamaica in 1938, providing a historiographical analogue to Collins's critique of the Party in Grenada. That is, he studies the tensions between popular and scholarly Marxist historiography of 1938 on the one hand and subaltern understandings of it on the other.

The remaining essays look at current or very recent events from across the Caribbean.

Sujatha Fernandes investigates emergent collectivities in Venezuela today, identifying their differences from traditional modes of Left organizing used by trade unionism, rural guerrilla warfare, or state-led mobilizations in the Cuban Revolution (or indeed in Venezuela). Fernandes's focus is the emergence in 2005-6 of a remarkable coalition of urban community-based media groups and rural indigenous groups to oppose new coal-mining projects in Zulia. Central to her analysis are the grounding contradictions between Venezuela's continued subjection to global capitalism and its projects for social reform; and between the concentration of power in the figure of Chávez and the unleashing of grassroots and direct action activism with its demands for accountability. For related projects, see Duno-Gottberg 2009; Harris 2007.

In a pan-Caribbean analysis, Norman Girvan, one of the key figures in the regional mobilization against the recent Economic Partnership Agreement between the EU and the Caribbean, provides a nuanced account of the likely consequences of the EPA, the efforts at mobilizing against it, and the primary reasons for the failure of that mobilization. While excellent studies of the fragmentation of the contemporary Haitian Left and the pressures under which it labors exist (see, for example, Dupuy 1996 and 2009), what is striking about Girvan's essay is its revelation that some of the most successful anti-EPA organizing took place in Haiti. Girvan also addresses the reasons for the muteness of mass-opposition to the EPA in the Anglophone Caribbean as compared with earlier anti-globalization agitations in Latin America.

The collection as a whole, but especially the two final essays by Alissa Trotz and Yarimar Bonilla, bring into focus through contrast the tremendously diverse sites, range, and registers of grassroots radicalism in the region. Trotz's essay focuses on how the feminist methodologies employed by the Red Thread collective in Guyana organized with women across race to respond to the devastating 2005 floods in ways quite different from traditional philanthropic conceptions of 'relief work', and in ways that counted women's caring labor. Bonilla's essay investigates an eruption of protest on a scale rarely seen in recent Francophone Caribbean history: the forty-four-day mass-strikes in Guadeloupe in 2009 that began with outrage over gas prices but soon developed into a list of 120 demands. She traces the emergence of the coalition *Lyannaj Kont Pwofitasyon* (roughly translated as the Alliance Against Profiteering) and the significance of the glimpse which the strike afforded of transformed social relations when the import-based economy was interrupted. The methods and conjunctures these two essays dwell upon are different: Trotz's essay draws attention to the steady daily labor that quietly chips away at and transforms women's understandings of themselves, their work, and their social relations; Bonilla looks at a spectacular and intense instance of the discovery and exercise of collective power in crisis. But both participate in the same hunger. And, like Bogues and Fernandes, both emphasize collectives that cannot be axiomatically assumed ('the sisterhood of women', 'labor') but are prefigured or forged in practice.

The essays in this collection are wide-ranging in their interests; various in their styles of critique and in their focus on states, civil society, or markets; multi-lingual in their objects of analysis and in their original composition; and multidisciplinary. I have chosen not to smooth over or mute these discontinuities, in the belief that their dissonances point to some of the necessary difficulty of a necessary Caribbean Studies.

Besides bringing together scholarship from the social sciences and the humanities, this volume also features the work of two visual artists. The selections featured here from the work of the Barbadian artist Annalee Davis include photographs of her installation art as well as a still from her experimental documentary video. Davis's work embodies critiques of neoliberalism and its impact on Caribbean sovereignties; and it explores discrimination by Caribbean states against undocumented migrant labor from elsewhere in the Caribbean, visually expressing the 'tangled intimacy' of Caribbean relations to which I have referred. Kathy Sloane's photographs lovingly portray ordinary Caribbean people in their everyday lives, while also visually evoking the collective political contexts in which their lives are embedded.

The urgency of the efforts represented in this collection clearly stems from a very different kind of moment from that of 1 January 1959, when the Cuban Revolution triumphed, and when to many socialists, intellectuals, and disenfranchised people – peasants, working class, lumpenproletariat, around the world – all things seemed possible. Different, too, from the hopes of a unified Caribbean Federation, first glimpsed as reality just over fifty years ago, a Federation that failed in one historical iteration, but lives on stubbornly as a dream.

Ours is a different conjuncture also from 1989, when the USSR crumbled, different from the long decade of crisis and retreat that the global Left faced after that. (Though even this rough periodization conceals as much as it reveals. 1989 was also the year of the anti-IMF riots in Caracas. The subsequent twenty years have seen a weakening of the IMF's grip on Latin America.).

The current global crisis of capitalism which manifested itself in the crash of September 2008, is scarcely an occasion for Left triumphalism, but it must surely bring into yet sharper view that the planet itself cannot sustain current levels of consumption and waste; that 2% of the world's population owns over 50% of household wealth and that half the world's population combined owns only 1% of global wealth (United Nations Press Conference 2006); that hundreds of millions go hungry and do not have access to clean water; that half the world's population still lives on $2 a day; and that, as Claude Adams suggests, such a minimum wage demands maximum outrage (Adams 2009). If the early 1990's saw the Washington Consensus achieve hegemony, if ever we really resigned ourselves to global capitalism, to so-called 'TINA' ('There is no alternative'), that moment is surely not ours. Unless, that is, we redefine TINA to mean that *these* existing relations of power, *this* world order, *This* Is No Alternative.

The desperation that is driving food riots across the world, the strike demanding living wages in Guadeloupe and Martinique in 2009, massive anti-globalization and fair trade movements across the globe, the struggles for clean water, the rise to power through democratic electoral politics of Left parties across much of Latin America, the absence of certainties and hence also the release from dogma: all of these make ours a moment that is both sobering and inspiring. This, then, is a collective effort to remember the political landscapes we have jointly and separately walked, and to work our way towards a future more egalitarian, more just than the present.

Shalini Puri
Pittsburgh
2009

Acknowledgements:

Earlier versions of several of the papers collected in this volume were first presented at a colloquium entitled 'Remembering the Future: Radical Politics in the Caribbean', which was held at the University of Pittsburgh on 3-4 April 2009 with generous help from the College of Arts and Sciences and the Center for Latin American Studies, among others. Deep thanks to all the participants, and interlocutors who were present there, as well as to the other contributors to this volume. I am grateful to the referees of these essays for their rigorous commentaries. And finally, for the interest they took in this collection and the time they gave it, I thank the editors of *Interventions*, Robert Young, Rajeswari Sunder Rajan, and especially Alison Donnell.

References

Adams, C. (2009) 'Minimum Wage, Maximum Outrage', October 9, http://claudeadams.blogspot.com/2009/10/minimum-wage-maximum-outrage.html.

Beverley, J. (2009) 'Rethinking the Armed Struggle in Latin America', Special issue on the Sixties and the World Event. Eds. Chris Connery and Hortense Spillers. *boundary* 2 36.1, pp. 47-60.

Brathwaite, E. K. (1974) *Contradictory Omens: Cultural Diversity and Integration in the Caribbean*, Mona, Jamaica: Savacou Publications.

Chanan, M. (2004) *Cuban Cinema*, Minneapolis and London: University of Minnesota Press.

Duno-Gottberg, L. (2009) 'Mob Politics: Reconsidering Non-Traditional Social Movements in Contemporary Venezuela', Conference on 'Remembering the Future: The Legacies of Radical Politics in the Caribbean', University of Pittsburgh, 3-4 April.

Dupuy, A. (1996) *Haiti in the New World Order: The Limits of the Democratic Revolution*, Boulder, Colorado: Westview Press.

Dupuy, A. (2009) 'What is Left of the Left in Haiti after

Aristide?' Conference on 'Remembering the Future: The Legacies of Radical Politics in the Caribbean', University of Pittsburgh, 3-4 April.

Harris, J. (2007) 'Bolivia and Venezuela: The Democratic Dialectic in New Revolutionary Movements', *Race and Class* 49.1, pp. 1-24.

Keens-Douglas, P. (1986) 'Tell Me Again', ed. Paula Burnett. *The Penguin Book of Caribbean Verse in English*, New York: Penguin, pp. 56-58.

Scott, D. (2004) *Conscripts of Modernity: The Tragedy of Colonial Enlightenment*, Durham and London: Duke University Press.

United Nations Press Release, http://www.un.org/News/briefings/docs/2006/061205_Household_Wealth.doc.htm

RESONANCES OF REVOLUTION
Grenada, Suriname, Guyana

Rupert Roopnaraine
Working People's Alliance, Guyana

Editor's note
The author recalls his experience of the Grenada Revolution from the point of view of a key leader of the Working People's Alliance in neighbouring Guyana. What follows is a participant's account of how events in Grenada crossed and impacted unfolding developments on the Left in Guyana and Suriname. His recollections and analyses of the Grenada Revolution are thus filtered through the agitations against the dictatorship of Forbes Burnham in Guyana; the arson trial of Roopnaraine, Rodney and Omawale (1979–81); the assassination of Rodney (1980); the WPA's early links with Desi Bouterse who led the Sergeant's Revolt in Suriname (1980) and who seemed to offer a popular Left anti-imperialist and non-aligned path, and the hope of a break with ethnic politics; the 1982 killings by Bouterse's revolutionary government of 15 opposition leaders soon after a visit to Suriname by Grenada's Prime Minister Maurice Bishop; and finally, the author's mission to mediate the crisis in Grenada.

Grenada

The words of the history-making broadcast are by now well known. They are worth hearing again as we meet, thirty years later, to remember March 13th and what it came to mean:

> At 4:15 this morning, the People's Revolutionary Army seized control of the army barracks at True Blue.
>
> The barracks were burned to the ground. After half-an-hour struggle, the forces of Gairy's army were completely defeated, and surrendered.
>
> Every single soldier surrendered, and not a single member of the revolutionary forces was injured ...
>
> I am now calling upon the working people, the youths, workers, farmers, fishermen, middle-class people, and women to join our armed revolutionary forces at central positions in your communities and to give them any assistance which they call for ...
>
> In closing, let me assure the people of Grenada that all democratic freedoms, including freedom of elections, religious and political opinion, will be fully restored to the people ...
>
> People of Grenada, this revolution is for work, for food, for decent housing and health services, and for a bright future for our children and great-grandchildren. (Marcus and Taber 1983a)

As we huddled around the radio that day in March, drinking in the broadcasts being beamed out of Morne Rouge from the newly christened Radio Free Grenada, we could not have known, though we dared to imagine, the extent to which the events in a small Eastern Caribbean island would have electrified us all, nourishing and energizing the popular forces throughout the region and beyond; even less – far, far less – could we have foreseen the desolation and utter despair that settled like a dark lowering cloud when four years later the fratricidal blood-letting opened the way for Reagan's long-rehearsed invasion and the final destruction of the revolution.

In the atmosphere of the 1980s, the Grenada Revolution gave back to the Caribbean the sense of selfhood that Haiti had given it in the 1800s, albeit a selfhood all but obliterated in the prevailing conditions of slavery. Since Haiti in 1804 the Caribbean basin had borne witness to revolts, upheavals and periodic eruptions that culminated in the uprisings of the 1930s and the Cuban Revolution of 1959. Over the next two decades, the revolutionary tide had ebbed. The post-Independence English-speaking Caribbean, with their new flags and stirring anthems, seemed in the main to have settled down to a routine as takers rather than makers of history. But with the seizure of power by the Grenadian revolutionaries on 13 March the picture of kowtowing to power, of co-option into the upper classes, of comfortable Carib-Saxonship, was gone. The grandchildren of the enslaved were capable, like all oppressed humans, to resort to force and to use it with exemplary discretion.

It must be remembered that it was a bloodless or almost bloodless seizure of power. It showed a distinction between force and violence that history does not always permit. Brian Meeks, in his insightful *Caribbean Revolutions and Revolutionary Theory*, makes the point that

> Grenada's significance went far beyond its importance as a micro-state, because it was the first revolution carried out by black English-speakers, with direct lines of communication to the major black and West Indian population centres in North America and Great Britain and because it presented the United States for the first time since the Vietnamese War with an opportunity to reassert its hegemonic tendencies, by invading a state and overthrowing a regime which had already been shattered. (Meeks 2001: 2)

There could not have been a more direct line of communication than Maurice Bishop's speech to several thousand Americans at Hunter College in New York during his 1983 tour. Bishop drew attention to a 'secret report' of the State Department:

> That secret report made this point: that the Grenada revolution is in one sense even worse – I'm using their language – than the Cuban and Nicaraguan revolutions because the people of Grenada and the leadership of Grenada speak English, and therefore can communicate directly with the people of the United States. But I want to tell you what that same report said that also made us very dangerous. That is that the people of Grenada and the leadership of Grenada are predominantly Black. They said that 95 per cent of our population is Black – and they have the correct statistic – and if we have 95 per cent of predominantly African origin in our country, then we can have a dangerous appeal to 30 million Black people in the United States. Now that aspect of the report, clearly, is one of the most sensible. (Marcus and Taber 1983b)

For Fitzroy Ambursley, the armed seizure of power on 13 March 'represented the highest level of class struggle attained in the English-speaking Caribbean since the tumultuous slave uprisings of the seventeenth and eighteenth centuries' (Marable 1987: 223) Roy Neehal, a prominent Caribbean religious leader, writing on the significance of the revolution for the people of the region, made this assessment:

> One can understand why the Grenada revolution upset the dominant classes, the privileged minorities and the leaders of the establishment in the region. Here, for the first time, the poor and powerless masses were being given pride of place. Their needs, problems and aspirations became the *raison d'etre*, the central focus of policymaking, economic activity and social legislation.

Now, Caribbean governments and centres of power will find it harder to say to the masses that their hopes are idle dreams. (Neehal 1985: 103)

Encouragingly for another generation, it was a successful revolution of young people ready to take on the responsibilities of national reconstruction and world diplomacy.

The View from the Guyana Trenches

In the January issue of our party organ *Dayclean*, the Working People's Alliance was to declare 1979 the Year of the Turn: "Everything shows 1979 to be the Year of the Turn – from dictatorship over the masses to democracy of the masses; from scandal to decency; from shame to respect. With the people awake and rising it is possible for this turn to be a peaceful one, though powerful" (*Dayclean* 3.5). The party's analysis focused on the all-round deterioration of the living standards of the Guyanese working people in the period following the momentous events of the previous year, the victorious mass boycott of the fraudulent referendum on 10 July and the Jonestown massacre of 18 November, linking the treachery of the trade union leaders with the Great Poisoner: "When the workers rebelled within their unions, and some went on sickout, the greatest shame (before Jonestown) took place. The trade union leaders excited the masses by serving notice of a strike. Then BIG JIM called them to his throne and passed around the poison-cup. The rulers wanted the mass death of worker militancy. They did not succeed."

The January 1979 Year of the Turn analysis by WPA was prefaced by a stanza from our own Martin Carter's 1953 *Poems of Resistance*:

This is the dark time, my love,
It is the season of oppression, dark metal, and tears.
It is the festival of guns, the carnival of misery.
Everywhere the faces of men are strained and anxious.

We urged the Guyanese working people on to greater sacrifice and struggle in the year ahead. "At this point, WPA sends, the working people an old message: 'Continue to meet. Continue to talk serious trade union and serious politics. And ORGANIZE. This year you cannot avoid serious struggle. So organize. There is no other way. Organize as a class and then you can join with other forces. Organize.'" The publication closed with another stanza of Martin Carter's *Poems of Resistance*:

But I tell you
Like a tide from the heart of things

Inexorably and inevitably
A day will come.

And in the course of 1979, the day was to come in faraway Iran, in Nicaragua, and, close to home, in Grenada. In the wake of 13 March, the months ahead were to see the stirrings of revolt in other Eastern Caribbean territories. In Dominica, the sleaze-ridden government of Patrick John was forced to resign by a popular uprising on the streets of the capital. In St Lucia, that July, in an electoral revolt, the long-entrenched John Compton government was ousted after fifteen years in office, making way for the social democratic Labour Party. In the last month of the year, in St Vincent and the Grenadines, the newly formed United People's Movement, an alliance of three opposition parties including the socialist Youlou Liberation Movement, led by the now Prime Minister, Ralph Gonsalves, raised up a leftist challenge to the Milton Cato government. As its fright grew, the establishment became more and more hysterical. Cato's rabid anticommunist campaign evoked echoes of Georgetown in the turbulent 1960s. Catherine Sunshine records: "sound trucks patrolled the capital at 4 a.m. booming: 'Do not let the communists take over in St Vincent! If you vote UPM, you vote for communism! If you have two sheep, they'll take one! If you have one sheep, they'll cut it in half!'" (Sunshine 1985: 21).

It was a heady season of freedom and high hopes. As the months rolled by, the feeling took hold and grew: on 13 March 1979, the Caribbean people had taken a giant step into the future.

De Shah Gone! Gairy Gone! Who Next? Thus the banner headline emblazoned on the 30 March publication of *Dayclean Special* (3.6), later reproduced as a popular handbill and distributed around the city and the coast in the agitation that was to build into the civil rebellion of that year. It was later brandished by Burnham in the National Assembly to harangue and threaten the becalmed parliamentary opposition of Jagan's People's Progressive Party with the kind of violent friends they were consorting with. The dictator was not amused. There would be no emulation of the 13 March example of insurrection in Georgetown.

On 15 March the WPA cabled Caribbean governments and urged immediate recognition. When after six days there had still been no movement, we called again for the immediate recognition of the People's Revolutionary Government of Grenada: 'A good way to oppose the revolution in Grenada is to postpone recognition. Recognise and support it NOW. Do not sabotage the revolution. To delay is "foreign intervention."'

The Guyana dictator cannot be faulted for not recognizing the dangerous example. He took no chances. *Dayclean* records:

GEORGETOWN, GUYANA. Thursday, 15 March 1979 – The country is on full military alert. Military vehicles run up and down. Something is in the air. Police stations in the city, at least, have their gates locked. A guard is posted there to meet callers. Extra troops have been rushed to the extra residences of the Leader. There is a "joint command" of all the security forces. It is a military offence for soldiers to discuss what happened in Grenada on13 March.

The WPA, for its part, was not slow to identify the features we in Guyana shared with Grenada and to make a public call for the key lessons to be heeded in the struggle against a dictatorship that was growing more and more violent and repressive. The 20 March *Dayclean Special* on the overthrow of Gairy chose to highlight the following lessons:

- Within hours, a dictatorship which once looked like it couldn't be touched can be and was overthrown.
- When dictators use their power against the people, power has to be seized and taken back by any means necessary.
- The violence and thuggery of the tyrant cannot prevail against the armed people.
- The leadership of the revolution is entrusted to those in the front line of the resistance who become the special targets of the regime and pay a high price at the hands of its forces.
- Regional and international public opinion must be mobilized to expose the crimes of the dictator.
- The task is to build an alliance of all forces opposed to dictatorship and corruption.

These were not abstract lessons meant for all time and every place and the WPA did not intend them as such. They were directed to the actual conditions as they had been developing in Guyana over the years since Independence in 1966, when Forbes Burnham's People's National Congress was installed in power by the well-documented manoeuvres of the British and US governments acting in concert to dislodge and contain the pro-Soviet People's Progressive Party of Cheddi Jagan who, in the view of the cold warriors in Washington, was bent on creating 'another Cuba' in the hemisphere, a menace to be avoided at all costs. The flagrantly rigged elections of 1968 and 1973 had plunged Guyana into a social and political crisis that intensified with the rigging of the July 1978 referendum, which had the effect of closing and bolting the door to a peaceful constitutional change of government. By the time of the 13 March revolution in Grenada, the objective conditions were already ripening for popular revolt in Guyana. What, then, were the factors holding us back in the anti-dictatorial movement? What could Grenada teach us?

The lessons we chose to draw arose out of our experience in the intense battles of the sugar workers' strike of 1977 and the national mobilization against the referendum of 1978. In the face of an industrial rebellion that lasted 135 days in 1977 and a massively supported and vigorous boycott of the 1978 referendum, the Burnham dictatorship had bared its claws, unleashing a campaign of violence and intimidation against the workers and their unions, the opposition political parties and the democratic civil society organizations. In the civil rebellion that poured onto the streets of the capital following the early morning arrest of WPA leaders after the burning down of the Ministry of National Development and Office of the General Secretary of the PNC on the night of the first anniversary of the great referendum fraud, first the urban masses and then 'almost the whole society', in the words of Eusi Kwayana, 'were creeping out of the shadows into the light of hope once more, standing in defiance of the power that was extracting submission of their very self-respect, and imposing economic and financial oppression and hardship' (1988: 26). One of the ongoing tasks of the WPA that was spearheading the rebellion was to reinforce in the people their sense of their own gathering strength and of the dictatorship's fallibility and weakness. It was to this end that Walter Rodney so effectively used the weapon of ridicule against the dictator, the untouchable. It was a practicable application of lesson one of 13 March: *within hours, a dictatorship which once looked like it couldn't be touched can be and was overthrown.*

The importance we attached to the sixth lesson of 13 March – *The task is to build an alliance of all forces opposed to dictatorship and corruption* – had everything to do with the immense difficulties we were experiencing over many years in attempting to build an effective anti-dictatorial political unity. The failure to build such a unity was the single most disabling factor in the Guyanese struggle in the Year of the Turn. In my view, this failure not only prolonged the life of the dictatorship but emboldened it to embark on a programme of violence and repression that culminated in the assassination of Walter Rodney on 13 June 1980, almost one week to the day before the bomb exploded from under the speakers' platform at the rally to celebrate Heroes' Day at the Queen's Park Grandstand in St. Georges, directly below where five cabinet ministers of Grenada's People's Revolutionary Government were seated, killing three young women and injuring thirty-five persons.

At the start of the civil rebellion of 1979, the energy was on the streets and in the workplaces, not in the party councils. The building of a broad anti-dictatorial alliance had proven elusive. We in Guyana had not learned a key lesson of 13 March. And we paid and continue to pay the price.

Guyana Footnotes

> Progressives throughout the Caribbean were stunned by Bishop's arrest. From the UK, C.L.R. James sent a telegram to Coard and the NJM Political Bureau, stressing that Bishop's detention was 'an issue of importance not only to Grenada but the whole of the Caribbean, [which] must be solved through the mass of the population, unions and the Party. ... Primary is the safety of Bishop, for himself and the general public.' Rupert Roopnaraine of Guyana's Working People's Alliance and Michael Als of the Trinidadian People's Popular Movement attempted to negotiate between the factions. (Marable 1987: 259)

Because I have been mentioned in a number of dispatches, as the saying goes, I have decided to do what I have not done before outside the councils of the WPA and speak as fully as I can of my personal experience of the process, modest as it was, and in particular of its last days. I do so not to answer distortions put about in the immediate aftermath by one side in the dispute, but to set the record straight for the benefit of friends and comrades and for scholars as forward-looking and scrupulous as Manning Marable, from whom I lifted the above paragraph. In the end, for those of us who were in direct contact with the process and the leadership of the NJM, it is on that direct personal experience that we must draw if we are to make sense of a range of highly complex issues.

It was not until after the two-year-long arson trial ended on 30 May 1981 – with a dismissal of the charges against the three defendants (Omowale, myself and Walter Rodney, who had been assassinated a year into the trial) – that I was free to make my first visit to Free Grenada. Along with Andaiye, a fellow member of our Political Bureau and the party's International Secretary, we went as WPA delegates to the First International Conference in Solidarity with Grenada held in St George's from 23–25 November 1981. It was to be the first of many visits I and other party members were to make over the following two years. On that first occasion, Andaiye and I, and then I by myself, met long into the night with Maurice Bishop and Bernard Coard. We were one of the several delegations with whom they spent long hours in conversation over the course of the conference. Maurice talked laughingly about the abusive telephone call he had received from Burnham after the July 1979 burning down of the Ministry of National Mobilization, asking if he, Bishop, saw what his anarchist comrades in the WPA were up to in Georgetown. It was always something of a high-wire act for the NJM to maintain and manage fraternal relations with all three of Guyana's (at that time) main parties, two of which were waging a bitter fight against the third. Burnham – it is now well-enough known – had given active support to the NJM in the preparations for the assault on Gairy, even providing training for senior PRA officers in Guyana

Defence Force facilities in Guyana. Maurice spoke more somberly about Walter's assassination and the necessary harshness of the NJM statement in June 1980, and of Burnham's displeasure. In fact, Maurice had to repeat the statement that Walter Rodney had been assassinated after the PRG minister who came to the funeral was pressured into denying it.

It was the warmest and most comradely of sessions that night in November, and it marked the beginning of the WPA's active engagement with the NJM. Maurice's words as we were breaking up, just before dawn, have echoed in my mind ever since: 'If ever you come and I am not on the island, talk with Bernard. Talking to Bernard is the same as talking to me.' Over the next two years our relations with the NJM deepened, including the establishment of systems of communication and mutual assistance. The WPA sent delegations to Grenada to participate along with representatives of other Caribbean parties in the political education classes on Marxist-Leninist party building facilitated by the NJM and led by Trevor Munroe, then General Secretary of the Workers Party of Jamaica.

It must be admitted that the WPA was regarded as somewhat heretical in the congregation of orthodoxy that gathered in St Georges for the party-building workshops. As an independent Marxist party, we had not only long set our face against vanguardism – Guyana was already suffering from two established vanguard parties, Jagan's PPP and Burnham's PNC – but had compounded the heresy by institutionalizing co-leadership as a counter-example to the one-manism of the dictator we were fighting. I have been reminded by Andaiye (a member of our delegation to the workshop) that the WPA was not the only party that failed the test of rigid orthodoxy, with resistance coming from representatives from Antigua, Dominica and St Vincent. There were other tensions, latent to be sure, and in the light of the later open conflict, revealing in retrospect. In a rare visit to one of the sessions, Maurice Bishop gave his blessings to the need for organization, study, discipline and application, but cautioned against the belief that even the best designed workplans could be a substitute for the direct engagement with the masses. Although attempts to coordinate the struggles across the region did not get very far, there was more contact, more sharing of experience among the Left parties of the region than ever before. There was a sense of a single Caribbean project. All tendencies embraced the call pioneered by the NJM for the Caribbean to be a 'Zone of Peace'. The NJM was proud of the fact that they had succeeded in having the OAS assembly adopt a positive resolution on the Zone of Peace initiative in La Paz, Bolivia in 1979. It was a season of light, of renewal. Delegates returned to their theatres of operation invigorated and with a sense of a shared mission.

In the retreat that followed the collapse of the NJM and the explosion of inhumanity that signalled the death of the Grenada Revolution, many of the parties disappeared from view, with some of their members and leaders gravitating to the university campuses, the NGO movement or to the more mainstream political formations. In the grim disenchantment of the period, many turned their backs on political activity, never to be heard from again. At its members' conference in April 1984, the WPA formally abandoned the Leninist form of organization, dismantled the clandestine security units, and opted for the electoral path and the building of a mass party.

Apart from Maurice, with whom, as many others found, it was easy to share an instinctive comradeship that went beyond politics, the other member of the NJM leadership with whom I developed a close bond was Liam 'Owusu' James. My friendship with Owusu began and developed not in Grenada but in Paramaribo, where we would meet, or rather meet up, on a number of occasions, each on our own separate mission. Paramaribo was one of Owusu's assignments. I became the WPA's chief contact with the Surinamese military leadership.

Suriname Footnotes

Our relations with the Surinamese comrades were, by force of circumstance, initiated by Walter Rodney en route to Africa. Walter, before Guyana courts on the charge of arson, could only honour the invitation from ZANU-PF to attend the Zimbabwe Independence celebrations in April 1980 by discreetly leaving the jurisdiction of the court, and leaving behind the watchers of the Special Branch. Walter traveled overland along the coast and, in the dead of night, crossed the Corentyne River by speedboat into Suriname, where he was met by Surinamese activists and assisted on his way through to Amsterdam.

The WPA had welcomed Suriname's Sergeants' Revolt in February and saw it as opening the way to a new multi-racial progressive politics there. Badrissein Sital and Chas Mijnals, leaders of the Left faction in the National Military Council, were to participate in the historic 12 June Rodney Memorial Rally in Georgetown. Sital, then chairman of the Council, was one of the foreign visitors who addressed the rally. *Dayclean* of 19 June 1981, under the banner headline 'Empty pots and loaded guns', gives the flavour of the times:

> The memorial was a memorial to a victim of assassination who was also an outstanding freedom-fighter, and one close to the people's hearts. And visitors who came to Guyana, some of whom spoke at the rally, were happy to see the revolutionary attitude of the Guyanese masses, to see and hear their response to the discussion of serious political issues, to witness and experience the multi-racial character of the struggle, to see that the masses of Guyanese working people are proudly holding the Rodney banner of unity, hatred for oppression and boldness of

political thought and action. These visitors, one after the other, directed their solidarity not to any political party, but to the masses of Guyanese working people of all races, occupations, ages and faiths who stood before and around them in unity and determination. (*Dayclean* 6.7)

A section of the rally marched through the streets of the city, past the president's house, down to the spot of the fatal explosion of the year before, chanting for bread and justice. When confronted by the riot squad, they shouted, 'People's Power! No Dictator!', the chant with which Walter had electrified the country during the civil rebellion of 1979.

I was not present at the memorial rally. The previous week, having been prevented by Special Branch or one of its tentacles from exiting Guyana even after I had been freed by the courts, I had travelled along the Rodney route across the river into Suriname, where I was met by the comrades who once more extended their courtesies, enabling me to travel to Europe and participate, along with Pat Rodney, in the first anniversary commemoration activities in London and Hamburg. This was our second contact with the Surinamese revolutionaries. Later that year, one of the leading comrades of the RVP (*Revolutionaire Volkspartij*) paid me a visit at my home in Georgetown. It was the first daylight meeting of the WPA and the Surinamese revolutionary leadership. I recall him gently rebuking me for having told the packed audience at Conway Hall in London that I had travelled 'through the Walter Rodney airport'. He felt it had been a serious security breach and could give ammunition to the counter-revolutionary forces. It did not strike me as such at the time, but it has occurred to me since that one of the lessons of the Grenada tragedy is that it can be self-defeating to make a fetish of secrecy, especially when the likelihood is that the secrets are already in the possession of the enemy.

I was to have my first formal meeting with the leadership of the process when I attended and carried WPA's greetings and solidarity to the launching of the Revolutionary Front in Paramaribo in August 1981. This was the period of strongest Left influence after a lurch to the right the previous months. Sital, Mijnals and five other leftists who had been arrested in August 1980 and charged with conspiracy, were all released in March 1981. The expulsion of the small Dutch military mission was followed soon after by the opening of a Cuban embassy in Paramaribo. In July, a Surinamese delegation attended the SICLAC (Socialist International Latin American and Caribbean section) meeting in Grenada. Delegations to the launching of the Front in August came from Nicaragua, Cuba, El Salvador, Grenada and other Caribbean territories. By this time the scale had tipped decisively in favour of the parties of the Left, which began to play a leading role in the National Military Council and the government. The RVP and the PALU (*Progressieve*

Arbeiders en Landbouwers, Progressive Workers and Farmers Union) each had a minister in the cabinet.

Even in the midst of a situation of rising tensions in the country, Desi Bouterse, the army commander and leader of the revolution, agreed to provide logistical assistance to the WPA to mount a commando operation to extract Gregory Smith, the assassin of Walter Rodney, from his bolt-hole in Cayenne, French Guiana, and return him to stand trial in Georgetown. The extraction team was on its way to Cayenne on 8 December 1982 when the explosion of the crisis in Paramaribo forced the abortion of the operation. Gregory Smith and the authors of the conspiracy were improbable beneficiaries of the December 1982 killings in Suriname. He was to eventually die in Cayenne of natural causes.

Maurice Bishop's visit to Suriname in October 1982 occurred at a time of heightened tensions in Paramaribo, with the two major unions in the forefront of a campaign of spreading resistance to the Revolutionary Front and all its works. Provocations were met with repression that fuelled more demonstrations on the streets. C47, led by Fred Derby, who had participated in the Front in August of the previous year, and the Moederbond labour federation, led by the AIFLD trained Cyrill Daal, started by mobilizing their members on economic issues such as the rise in rice prices. The government and its supporters saw the campaign as an orchestration by right-wing counter-revolutionary forces to bring down the revolution and turn back the tide. And they treated it as such, with the invasion of the Moederbond's headquarters by the militia and the rising crescendo of charges and counter-charges. Healthcare and education workers came out on strike. It was into this turbulence that Maurice Bishop touched down in Paramaribo.

By design or not, the opportunity to humiliate Bouterse could not have been more inviting. Cyrill Daal had successfully organized the air traffic controllers' strike that almost prevented Bishop's plane from landing. He timed his protest rally to coincide with the mass gathering organized by the government to welcome Bishop. One account I have seen has Daal brushing aside Bouterse's invitation to the reception for Bishop, even colourfully insinuating that the order for Daal's subsequent arrest was also an act of pique. The arrest, after the weeks of thrust and counter-thrust, led to wider and larger protests and the downing of tools by workers at the power plant, much to the glee of the counter-revolutionary forces who gloated that Bouterse had to entertain his honoured guest by candlelight. The final provocation came on 30 October. Daal threw down the gauntlet by again timing his own mass rally to coincide with Bouterse's national rally for Bishop. Several reports claimed that Daal's rally was ten times the size of Bouterse's. To pour salt in the wound, Daal's address was broadcast live by the local radio station, ABC, which was owned by popular businessman and former Minister of Sports and Culture, Andre Kamperveen. By this time,

Derby, disturbed by Daal's increasingly confrontationist behaviour and the open politicization of the strikes, had put distance between himself and Daal, weakening the industrial front of the campaign. However, disagreement between the government and the unions over the date for a new constitution and national elections rekindled the protests and led to the closing of ranks among the opposition forces, including Derby's C47 and the Moederbond. On 31 October 1982, C47, together with the Progressive Workers Association and the Civil Service Association, issued the First Plan of Reconstruction for the return to democracy. The Moederbond came on board soon after Daal's release from prison. A cluster of religious, business and professional organizations, including the Bar Association and the Association of Medical Practitioners, came together to form the Association for Democracy, widening and consolidating the resistance to the regime. As the pressure on the government mounted, the rebellion spread to the university campus and secondary schools. On 2 December a demonstration of university lecturers and secondary school students was set upon by the security forces, causing revulsion in wide sections of society and deepening the isolation of the revolutionary leadership.

In the early hours of 8 December, a round-up of the most prominent protest leaders began. They were seized by units of the army and taken to Fort Zeelandia, the military headquarters. Within hours, several buildings in Paramaribo were fire-bombed and burnt to the ground: among them, the ABC radio station, the Moederbond headquarters and the offices of the newspaper *De Vrije Stem*. On the evening of 8 December, an official statement from the military high command declared 'the revolutionary leadership had succeeded in frustrating an attempted coup that was designed to restore the situation whereby a small economic elite would come to power and trample underfoot the interests of the workers, peasants and masses of our people'. It was announced that a number of suspects had been arrested and were being held for questioning and that 'some major focal points that were spreading alarm and were being used as centres for the counter-revolution ... had also been physically destroyed'. Over the next few hours, fifteen of those in custody were executed. Rambocus, Daal and Kamperveen were among the military officers, lawyers, university professors and businessmen who were shot. Alone among the detainees, Fred Derby's life was spared.

On the night of 9 December, Bouterse announced on television that the prisoners had been shot while attempting to escape.

The December 1982 killings in Suriname sent shock waves around the Caribbean and beyond. In a statement issued on 5 November 1982, at the height of the campaign of strikes and protests, the WPA, remembering the role played by the AIFLD and the CIA in the Guyana strikes and disturbances of the early 1960s, had refused to rule foreign intervention out of the equation in Paramaribo. We hailed the visit of Maurice Bishop to Suriname as an important step in breaking the isolation between the English- and Dutch-speaking Caribbean territories. The rightist forces were not slow in laying the blame for the killings at the door of the Cuban and Grenada inspired socialist politics of the regime. 'These left-wing ideologies', wrote Caroline Wentzel,

> were nevertheless not supported throughout the whole of Suriname; military officials, politicians and the people themselves turned on Bouterse and his ideas. Grenada's Maurice Bishop had given Bouterse the advice to eliminate the powers that were against him or else they would eliminate him. Bouterse took this advice to heart and eliminated those who were against him. In conclusion, radical politics and personal interest resulted in the murders of 8 December 1982.

Shaken though it was by the inhumanity and bloodshed of December, on the third anniversary of the revolution, the WPA issued a statement maintaining its faith in the ideals of 25 February 1980:

> True to our conviction that it is the friends of a revolution who have the duty to point out its shortcomings, our party has informed the authorities in the neighbouring republic of its concerns at excesses involving the loss of life and the type of reactions to provocation that threaten due process. ... Our party is confident that the February 25th leadership will benefit from the three years of experience and overcome the frequent interruptions of the democratization process. ... Our party looks forward to the formation of the new government and wishes the revolution an uninterrupted period of peace and stability so that the neglect and dislocations of the centuries can be redressed and the relations among the Surinamese people can be radically altered in overwhelming favour of the oppressed and the disinherited. (*Open Word* 56, 28 February 1983)

In my researches for this presentation, I could not avoid consulting *Grenada Documents: An Overview and Selection*, the 'few hundred pages out of tens of thousands', spoils of war plundered from Grenada and published by the Department of State and the Department of Defense. There in Document 86, page 3, Item 2.7 of the Minutes of the Political Bureau of Wednesday, 22 December 1982, headed *Suriname Report*, I find the following:

> Comrade Layne gave the Bureau a very brief report on the situation in Suriname based on a word of mouth report he himself had received from Cde. Rupert Roopnaraine. The situation there was described as 'dreadful', with clear evidence of the involvement of the Dutch, British, Canadians and Americans; inability to work with the masses was also noted.
>
> Cde. Roopnaraine was due to attend PB at 1.30 for the purpose of a more detailed report. (Department of State 1984, Document 86: 3)

I could find no record of the 'detailed report' I made to the NJM leadership that afternoon in St Georges, although I am sure that I would have placed greater stress than Comrade Layne's brief report indicated on the widespread disaffection among the people and the excesses and isolation of the Surinamese revolutionaries.

Grenada: Thirteen Days in October

We were assembled at the WPA Party School in Georgetown for our weekly party-building classes when the news reached us late on 13 October that Maurice Bishop had been placed under house arrest. We were stunned. Fraternal parties in the region with which we were in contact had a similar reaction. Nothing in our close and deep relationship with the NJM at all levels had given us any inkling of the divisions in the party that were tearing it apart. The WPA dispatched a cable to the NJM:

> Political Bureau in session conveys to NJM our confidence that revolution will seize space within principles apparently in dispute in interest mainly of working people's morale in this hour of reactionary counter-vigilance in region, and will establish revolutionary composition of issues to permit continued examination. Respectfully and fraternally request circulation of this message. (*Dayclean* 8.34)

In our assessment a few months later, on 13 March 1984, the WPA was to identify this iron secrecy as one of the elements that contributed to the disaster:

> The very real external threat to the revolution gave rise to a siege mentality inside it and led the NJM to insist on the tightest secrecy concerning its internal differences. Ultimately, it turned out that it was unhelpful that the NJM concealed from its fraternal parties in the region the split in its leadership and the nature of that split which, contrary to what the WPA thought at first, did include elements of a power struggle, or did become a power struggle. More unfortunately, the rank and file membership of the NJM itself was kept in the dark until the eleventh hour. (WPA, 'Grenada and the Caribbean', 13 March 1984)

Some time on 14 October I received a telephone call from Grenada conveying a request from the NJM Central Committee to come immediately to the island to help in resolving the conflict. The WPA leadership agreed to accept the invitation and instructed that I do nothing until after I had first spoken to Maurice. On my way to Grenada, I over-nighted in Port of Spain, as I usually did, at the home of Alan Alexander, the veteran labour lawyer who had been my counsel in our defence team at the arson trial and had become a close and trusted friend and comrade. Alan had long been a close friend of Maurice, a colleague in the Caribbean progressive legal fraternity in the 1970s. (He had been appointed Chairman of the Constitution Commission established by the PRG in June 1983 to draft a new constitution that would include provisions for regular elections.) It was one of the occasions we talked through the night on the verandah high above the valley in Margarita. Our conversation had not been so sorrowful since June 1980 when we lost Walter. I tried to persuade Alan to accompany me to Grenada, knowing the standing he enjoyed with the comrades. But Alan had too deep a sense of foreboding. He hoped my efforts would succeed, but he felt that the situation had become too far out of control and the signs were not hopeful. I should be careful.

I arrived at Pearls Airport in the middle of the morning of 17 October and went by taxi to the home of my parents, who had been living in St Georges for the past two years. Later that afternoon Owusu came over. I relayed the instructions I had been given by the WPA: to speak with Maurice before I did anything else. I asked that he arrange the meeting. He returned later that evening with copies of the minutes of the Central Committee and General Members' Meetings which he asked me to study. He was working on the arrangements for me to meet with Maurice and hoped it could happen the following day. I was assigned two security officers, who remained on the premises. Tuesday came and went without contact, except for a phone call from Owusu to say that things were very tense and difficult, but that he was still working on the arrangements. Hopefully, I would see Maurice the next day. He advised that I stay off the streets. I passed the hours at home reading the party minutes and following the events as best as I could from the announcements on Radio Free Grenada and phone calls from residents and friends. There was a large contingent of Guyanese living in Grenada and working at all levels of the state and society.

The following day, Wednesday the 19th, pandemonium broke out as the revolution exploded on to the streets. The events of the day have been prolifically documented, with the understandably different weightings and finger-pointing – the mass mobilization, the storming of the house to release Maurice, the triumphant march he set out to lead to the market square where thousands had assembled and were waiting, the fateful diversion to the fort, the battle at the fort, and the murders. The discharge of heavy guns and exchange of automatic fire were loud from across the valley. The guns fell silent. The hush was then broken by a single burst of machine gun fire. I learned long afterwards that the hush had lasted for all of twenty minutes; that afternoon it seemed very much shorter. Later in the afternoon Owusu called on the telephone. The situation was tense but under control. To my question, 'How is Maurice?' Owusu corrected my tense. 'How *was* Maurice you mean.' Thirty years on, I find Owusu's response no less chilling than I did that afternoon in St Georges.

The morning after, Michael Als (leader of the Trinidadian People's Popular Movement) brought me a message from the Central Committee. It was then that I learned that Als had been mediating between Maurice and the Central Committee and had met with the CC members and then with Maurice on the afternoon of Tuesday the 18th. I wondered then and have wondered since if it had been the WPA's insistence on a meeting with Maurice as a precondition of our mediation that ruled us out as mediators. Als described Maurice as sweating and smoking a lot. The comrades were asking that I hold a press conference when I arrived in Barbados confirming that Maurice and the others had been shot in crossfire at the fort. I sent back the response that since I was not present at the fort I was in no position to speak on what had happened. I cannot say whether or not my response was delivered, but I received no further requests. Up to this point I had not set foot outside the house, but was to do so for the first time the following day when I was driven up to Fort Frederick to meet with Bernard Coard. Everyone was in military fatigues. There was a frenzy of preparations for defence against the invasion that was threatening. To my question how could we in the WPA have been kept in the dark about what was going on in the NJM, he chuckled about how well they kept their secrets. We then spoke mainly of possible arrangements to get me off the island. The airport would soon be closed. Bernard felt that a boat to Carriacou and from there to Barbados should be considered. He obviously had more pressing things on his mind. He worried about a run on the banks.

As the hours went by and the harsh curfew was imposed by the newly arisen Revolutionary Military Council, led by army chief Hudson Austin, the prospect of invasion loomed. I watched the young brothers and sisters of the PRA and the militia heading off into the mountains. I volunteered to do what I could to assist, a decision that opened me to the charge of giving support to the murderers of Maurice, Jackie and the others, and was to require explanation when I eventually returned to Georgetown. I say now what I said then: when it came to the physical defence of the island against the invading US forces, it would have been dishonourable to do otherwise. I was issued with a Makarov semi-automatic, a car and military driver, and assigned to Telephone House, where I was asked to monitor calls between the American medical students and their relatives in the USA. I was also asked to make telephone contact with fraternal parties in the region to keep them abreast of the advancing invasion. From the Friday to the eve of the invasion, from early morning to late at night, I listened in to the telephone conversations and spoke with comrades around the region. I sent my daily reports to the military command. All the while, I was to discover later, the WPA was making frantic efforts to get me off the island. After the spirited resistance ended after four days and nights, and through the intervention of Lord Avebury and the British High Commission, my mother and I were included in the airlift of UK citizens (I was travelling on my UK passport) off the island in a C-130. After being processed by the new US army immigration service, we arrived at Barbados airport, which had been converted into a massive launch pad with F16s and helicopter gunships from end to end. I arrived in Guyana on the night of the 30th and was held for questioning at the airport by Special Branch.

After my report to the WPA Central Committee, the party issued the following statement with its 'Ten points on Grenada'. For purposes of the record, I reproduce it in full:

1.   When the WPA heard of the problems in the NJM on 14 October, we sent a cable asking for compromise and we sent a member to help. On 19 October, when soldiers of the People's Revolutionary Army and Bishop and others met their deaths, it was difficult to understand what had happened or to accept the military council's explanations. The WPA said, before our members' return, that we were sickened by the killings and could find no justification or explanation to excuse those who were responsible for the act.

Our two members who were in Grenada separately have now returned. After listening to their reports, the WPA has arrived at certain conclusions. *Dayclean* wishes to state some of these, and repeat or correct certain important points.

How did Bishop and the other five leaders meet their deaths? The crisis in the NJM was longstanding and deep-rooted. It is now clear that the party had no rules to deal with the emergency when it arose and that terrible errors were committed by everyone involved. When Maurice Bishop was placed under house arrest, the masses understandably became agitated, especially when they were only hearing the party's side of the dispute. The party was very angry with Maurice Bishop for his part in circulating the ugly rumour about the Coards wishing to kill him. The Central Committee was satisfied that the accusation against the Coards was untrue and wicked. When Maurice Bishop was released from house arrest, he either went to Fort Rupert or was swept along by the crowd. Many in the crowd were genuine supporters, but there were also enemies of the revolution who seized the opportunity for mischief. At the fort, guns were shared out. When the army arrived to retake the fort, three soldiers were killed. The military accused Maurice Bishop and the five leaders of being responsible for the deaths of the soldiers and for taking people into the fort and giving them guns. Maurice and the others were not killed in crossfire after the soldiers were killed. They were arrested and then killed.

2.   It is the opinion of the WPA that whatever difficulties the NJM or the army found themselves in, the execution of Maurice Bishop and others is not excusable.

3.   The facts as they emerge do not support any conspiracy theory.

4.   The invasion of Grenada had been planned and rehearsed long in advance by Reagan. Remember Amber and the Amberines, the exercise carried out right here

in the Caribbean. However, the killing of Bishop and the others weakened the Grenadian people and made it easier for Reagan.

5.   The heads of states of the OECS countries, Jamaica and Barbados are guilty of high treason and murder against the Caribbean nation.

6.   Grenadians did fight to defend their country against the US invading force. The army (PRA) and a small section of the militia fought bravely. The military was not at its full strength for several reasons. After the killing of Maurice Bishop, the military council disarmed the militia in many places. Because the leader they loved had been killed and because the military council did not tell the truth about the killing, only about 1,500 of the militia turned out. At its high point earlier this year, the militia strength was about 15,000. When the military council took control on 19 October and then began to warn of an invasion, people believed that it was part of a cover-up, especially when the invasion did not come on Monday morning, the 24th, as predicted by the radio. When it did come the next morning, Tuesday 25 October, many were taken by surprise. Some who attempted to join their units on the night of the 25th could not because of transportation and other difficulties. The army quite early gave instructions for its members to change into civilian clothing, but many soldiers did not get the word and kept on fighting.

7.   Did Grenadians welcome the invasion? The troops arrived so swiftly after the tragic events of 19 October that many in their distress, did. Many were saying, 'No Maurice, no revolution'. In some of the most depressed areas where the revolution was not yet able to win over the people with social and economic benefits, the troops found support. Gairy's men were released from prison. These criminals and other enemies of the revolution, overjoyed by 19 October, certainly supported the invaders. However, there were many who gave secret support to the army and militia.

8.   The WPA finds the attempt of the US invading forces and its lackeys in the Caribbean to frame the Cuban people and government, vulgar. We see it as Reagan's further preparation for further slaughter in the Caribbean and Central America. When the US military headquarters realized that their lies against Cuba were exposed, they admitted that the figures given by the Cuban government about the number of Cubans on Grenada were accurate. Most of the Cubans were construction workers at the new airport.

9.   The WPA holds firmly to the view that Maurice Bishop as revolutionary leader of free Grenada was a shield protecting Grenada and the entire Caribbean. He held higher than any the banner of the Caribbean as a Zone of Peace. This banner should be taken up by all peace-loving people, in our own interest and in his memory.

10.   Finally, we believe that the tragic events of 19 October in Grenada raise a question that all serious parties will have to face: whether or not differences which develop inside the party should be put for public discussion before they get out of hand. (*Dayclean* 8.36)

This final conclusion was one of those quoted with approval in Gordon Lewis's *Grenada: The Jewel Despoiled* (1987), which remains to my mind one of the keenest and most honestly researched of the many scholarly and not so scholarly treatments of the upheavals I have been able to consult. Which is not to say that some of Lewis's interpretations of the party dispute are not open to question. From then to now, we have been in the presence of competing narratives of the end of the revolution. The explanation that I find the most persuasive is the one provided by Brian Meeks in his *Caribbean Revolutions and Revolutionary Theory*. Rejecting theories of conspiracy and a long-hatched and well-designed power struggle, Meeks identifies instead the collision of the two diverging logics that had been present in the NJM from the outset: the logic of the vanguard party and the logic of the supreme leader. 'It is my belief', Meeks writes, 'that there was no substantial ideological or tactical differences and, although personality did, of necessity, intercede, the overarching issue was the growing disconnection of the leadership *tout court* from the people, which, coupled with the depth of the crisis and the physical strain of paternalist rule, drove them to take irretrievable decisions' (2001: 166). Thirty years on, progressive opinion in the Caribbean, and not only in the Caribbean, remains divided. No issue has traumatized and divided the Left more deeply. We were divided inside and among parties. The scars are still with us. Gordon Lewis's words written more than twenty years ago hold true to this day:

> The real post-mortem had to deal with the fact that October 1983 was in large part a self-inflicted wound of the revolution itself. It thus became necessary, and it is still necessary, for the progressive movement, in the best spirit of democratic self-criticism, without nostalgia or evasive apologetics or scapegoating, to ask, and to seek to answer, the crucial questions: what went wrong in the internal dynamics of the revolution, why did things go wrong, and what are the long-term implications for the Caribbean revolutionary cause in the future? (Lewis 1987: 161)

All things considered and in all the circumstances as we came to know them, the WPA was to conclude:

> The explosion of the Grenada revolution onto the streets in October 1983, its self-exposure, its unconscious injustices, its over-rating, even to the very end, of its capacity to protect its reputation, its beautiful and attractive advocacy of internationalism and its rejection of internationalism in crucial areas, the high-minded principles it defended and abused at the same time, its making the majority within the vanguard a fetish and ignoring the majority among the masses: this is an act of depoliticization of the peoples of the region which cradled it. Disenchantment is the chief resulting emotion.

While the controversy over the end endures, and narratives continue to compete, there is no dispute over the beginning and the unfolding of the process over the four and a half years of its existence. 'For all that it did wrong, the PRG leadership was able to mobilize a mass enthusiasm for the revolution that no other Caribbean country save Cuba has managed to do' (Lewis 1987: 198). The achievements of the revolution in the areas of healthcare, housing, and in particular education, have been thoroughly documented and are beyond dispute: the free medical and dental care provided through a network of rural clinics to people who previously had no access to healthcare, the distribution of hot school lunches to children and milk to mothers and infants, the revolving loan fund to help the poor to repair their homes, the voluntary literacy programme aimed at the elimination of adult illiteracy and the programme of in-service training aimed at upgrading the skills of Grenadian primary school teachers. This concentration on the satisfaction of basic needs, along with a recovering economy led by an expanded state sector, has been rightly hailed as the most impressive achievement of the revolution. In four short years, the dilapidated slum that the PRG inherited from Gairy was being transformed from the bottom up and life for the majority of the population, the poor and the powerless, was being measurably improved.

We are at one with those commentators who have identified the democratic impulse that released the creativity and genius of tens of thousands of Grenadians at the grassroots who for the first time anywhere in the Caribbean became the active agents of their own betterment, what Meeks (2001) called 'an almost tangible revolutionary spirit, which tapped under-utilized energy, inspired the beginnings of a cultural revolution and raised the self-esteem of ordinary Grenadians at home and abroad'. This he rightly saw as a 'rekindled sense of self and of possibility'. To move this process of decentralization and popular mobilization forward, the zonal and parish councils were established to bring the people directly into the process of decision-making. This was entirely consistent with the NJM 1973 Manifesto that took over from its most ideologically developed constituent organization, the Movement for the Assemblies of the People (MAP), the position that emphasized the decentraliza-tion of state structures through a system of village assemblies. The manifesto called for nothing less than the reconstruction of the state from the base up. Merle Hodge and Chris Searle, both internationalist workers in Grenada, overwrite enthusiastically of the 'courageous democratic initiatives' that had taken hold across the island:

> Up to 13 March 1979, 'Parliament' used to be a barricaded building in town, York House, where fifteen men from the better-off sections of society met at Gairy's whim to hold debates and take decisions about the affairs of a nation of 110,000 people.
>
> Today in Grenada, Parliament has moved out of town and into the communities. Government has escaped out of York House and spread into community centres,

school buildings, street corners, market places, factories, farms and workplaces around the country. Political power has been taken out of the hands of a few privileged people and turned over to thousands of men, women and youth, of all walks of life, in every nook and cranny of Grenada, Carriacou and Petite Martinique. (Hodge and Searle n.d.: 22)

Given the growing pains the process experienced, and the inevitable tensions that developed between the inclusive assemblies and the exclusive vanguard party, the new democratic institutions, still in their infancy, may not have been that unqualified a success. But at its best, as in the budget consultations in 1982 and 1983, it marked the first serious attempt in the English-speaking Caribbean to dismantle the authoritarian colonial state and create a genuine participatory democracy. Bernard Coard described in a pamphlet of the time how the new process worked:

Many new programmes of the Revolution were conceived or 'born' in the Parish Council meetings – the National Transport Service (NTS) being the first such example, in the very early days of the Assemblies starting up. Many specific economic (including taxation) measures were first suggested by the people in these Assemblies. And many roads, drains, main water pipes, sewage disposals, feeder roads for farmers, health and maternity clinics, etc. got repaired or installed or constructed ... as a direct consequence of the interaction of the masses in the Assemblies with the politicians, civil servants and state managers. (Hart 2005: 7)

I am not alone in thinking that had the party conflict been taken out of the airless hothouse of the Central Committee and brought into the open air of the zonal and parish councils for resolution, the course of Grenadian and Caribbean history might well have been altogether different.

And herein lies what may well have been the revolution's greatest sin: to hold out the promise of the ordinary people taking direct control of their destiny, devising the strategies of their own development, holding those who would be leaders and representatives to account. For the most part, it seems safe to say that the necessary lessons have been learned from the fatal errors of October. In the words of my colleague in the WPA, Clive Thomas, 'after Grenada, no social project carried out in the name of the masses of the Caribbean peoples, whether by government or opposition, will receive widespread support from the popular forces and their organizations if it does not clearly embrace political democracy in its norms of political conduct' (Thomas 1984).

So, where do we go from here? The post-Independence neocolonial state forms, give or take a few amendments here and a few perversions there, are still very much with us in the Caribbean, sitting on top of the masses of the people, choking off their energies, thwarting popular initiatives, damming the flow of ideas and creativity. Writing in the *New African* in February

2009, the distinguished man of letters from Ghana, Ayi Kwei Armah, surveyed the current African scene and spoke for more than Africa:

> At the time of independence, Africa's rulers had the option of abolishing that obsolete, inherently anti-democratic, and always deadly system. Instead, they chose to sacralize it. ... In the euphoria surrounding independence, no one worried unduly how a system so demonstrably anti-democratic could suddenly become democratic because African politicians had replaced European administrators at the top. (Armah 2009: 32–7)

'...and for a bright future for our children and great-grandchildren'

The perception has been for some time growing across the Caribbean that the existing state forms inherited at Independence disable the Caribbean people from overcoming the scourge of poverty and underdevelopment. Calls for constitutional reform are increasing as the weaknesses of the present system become more and more glaring, except to its gatekeepers and stakeholders. The task is to build grassroots change-oriented organization in and out of parties on the basis of practical and strategic issues and in a spirit of non-sectarian inclusivity. The experience of Grenada has delegitimized vanguard-ism and instructs that it is more imperative than ever to build alliances across differences. We must learn the strength of otherness and difference and, above all, we must guard against the fatal arrogance of righteousness. We must focus on what we agree on and work persistently and with integrity on differences that are primary contradictions. The community based organizations outside the political parties are already networking for health, literacy, child protection, environmental sanity and disaster preparedness, against family violence and rape. We must deepen the work, multiply and connect these networks within and across territories. In a recent letter to me on how he saw the new possibilities, my friend and comrade of long standing, the Rodneyist historian Horace Campbell, wrote: 'In practical terms the networks of networks form the kernel of the new move for revolutionary organization. These networks provide spaces for self-awareness, self-mobilization, and self-organization for the tasks at hand. Quantitatively, the more of these networks, the more possibility for the leap.' The progressive parties and networks have the duty to transform irresponsible personal and community behaviours, to mount and sustain vigorous modern campaigns within and across the territories of the region, reinforced by diasporic resources and energies, to reform the unaccountable and unrepresentative electoral systems, the disempowered local government systems and the heavily centralized national governmental systems. Because elections are the only road available, broad-based movements rooted in the communities and traditional civil society organizations must prepare themselves to enter the electoral arena and launch a people's challenge to the old politics and its entrenched interests, armed with a radical and humane social, economic and political reform agenda, with the dismantling of the ossified state system as the number one priority. Only such a root and branch transformation of the state will bring our Caribbean societies closer to the ideals of free Grenada, where men and women once dreamed of a better life for their children and great-grand-children, confident that no challenge could not be overcome when the power to take charge of their lives rests in the hands of the ordinary people.

Acknowledgements

This essay was first presented at the conference 'Remembering the Future: The Legacies of Radical Politics in the Caribbean' at the University of Pittsburgh, 5 April 2009.

References

Armah, A. K. (2009) 'African elections: ending the violence', *New African* 481: 32–7.

Brizan, G. (1984) *Grenada, Island of Conflict: From Amerindians to People's Revolution, 1498–1979*, London: Zed Books.

Coard, B. (2002) *Summary Analysis of the October, 1983 Catastrophe in Grenada*. Unpublished.

Hart, R. (2005) *The Grenada Revolution: Setting the Record Straight*, London: Caribbean Labour Solidarity and Socialist History Society, Occasional Papers Series.

Hodge, S. and Searle, C. (n.d.) *'is freedom we making': The New Democracy in Grenada*, St George's, Grenada: Government Information Service.

Kwayana, E. (1988) *Walter Rodney*, Georgetown: Working People's Alliance.

Latin American Bureau (1984) *Grenada: Whose Freedom?* London: Latin American Bureau.

Lewis, G. K. (1987) *Grenada: The Jewel Despoiled*, Baltimore: Johns Hopkins University Press.

Marable, M. (1987) *African and Caribbean Politics from Kwame Nkrumah to Maurice Bishop*, London: Verso.

Marcus, B. and Taber, M. (eds) (1983a) 'A bright new dawn', in *Maurice Bishop Speaks: The Grenada Revolution 1979–1983*, New York: Pathfinder, p. 24.

Marcus, B. and Taber, M. (eds) (1983b) 'Maurice Bishop speaks to US. Working People', in *Maurice Bishop Speaks: The Grenada Revolution 1979–1983*, New York: Pathfinder, p. 299.

Meeks, B. (2001) *Caribbean Revolutions and Revolutionary Theory: An assessment of Cuba, Nicaragua and Grenada*, Mona, Jamaica: UWI Press.

Meeks, B. (2007) *Envisioning Caribbean Futures: Jamaican Perspectives*, Mona, Jamaica: UWI Press.

Neehal, R. (1985) 'Significance of the Grenada Revolution for the people of the Caribbean', in C. A. Sunshine (ed.) *The Caribbean: Survival, Struggle and Sovereignty*, Washington, DC: Epica, p. 103.

People's Revolutionary Government (1982a) *Grenada Is Not Alone*, St George's, Grenada: Fedon Publishers.

People's Revolutionary Government (1982b) *'To Construct from Morning – Making the People's Budget in Grenada*, St George's, Grenada: Fedon Publishers.

Sunshine, C. A. (1985) *The Caribbean: Survival, Struggle and Sovereignty*, Washington, DC: Epica.

Thomas, C. (1984) 'Hard lessons for intellectuals', *Caribbean Contact* (September): 12.

US Department of State and Department of Defense (1984) *Grenada Documents: An Overview and Selection*, Washington, DC: Government Printing Office.

Wentzel, C. (n.d.) 'The 8 December murders in Surinam and United States reactions during the early 1980s.' Unpublished dissertation.

ARE YOU A BOLSHEVIK OR A MENSHEVIK?

Mimicry, Alienation and Confusion in the Grenada Revolution

Merle Collins

University of Maryland, USA

A Personal Response to the Grenada Events of October 1983

The period that has come to be known as the Grenada Revolution began on 13 March 1979, the day the New Jewel Movement (NJM) took control of the Grenada government, and came to an end on 25 October 1983, the day the United States invaded Grenada. Or some might say it ended on 19 October 1983, the day when differences within the party created the implosion that led to the murders of Prime Minister Maurice Bishop, Foreign Minister Unison Whiteman, Minister of Education Jacqueline Creft, Minister of Health and Housing Norris Bain, trade union leader and ex-Central Committee member Vincent Noel, Fitzroy Bain, also once a member of the NJM Central Committee, and others – Evelyn Bullen, Keith Hayling, Evelyn Maitland, Andy Sebastien Alexander, Simon Alexander, Gemma Belmar, Eric Dumont, Avis Ferguson, Alleyne Romain and Nelson Steele. These are the names listed in a monument at Fort George (also Fort Rupert), the place where party members and others were killed in the final intra-party blooding. I am always struck by the perception that there may be others not named, and this is important to me partly because the end revealed such elitism in a political party that started off avowedly democratic in intent that it would be a particular injustice to name the elites of the party and not honor all others who were killed.

The bloody demise of the Grenada Revolution left a bitter after-taste in the Caribbean palate, distaste for any experiments that did not conform to models inherited from the British colonials.

In a January 2009 interview with a local Grenadian television station, NJM Central Committee member John (Chalkie) Ventour, who was released in December 2008 after spending 25 years in prison for complicity in the murders of his party comrades, apologized for dashing 'the hopes and aspirations' of so many people:

> I want to apologize for this. On behalf of my comrades who are still in prison, the surviving leaders of the revolution and all those who have died, I want to apologize for this. (Ventour 2009)

Ventour acknowledged that sometimes 'revolutionary movements create as much repression as they set out to solve' and, implicitly, he put the Grenadian revolutionary movement in that category.

How did a group of people, showing every appearance of unity and determination to succeed in transforming their small island society when their party seized office in 1979, arrive at a place of internecine strife by 1983? How did these political dreamers ever get to the stage where one side could be accused of murdering the other?

This essay presents a very personal response – some thoughts related to the questioning I did in the years immediately following the demise of the revolution. Let me declare my personal interest in this discussion. As a young person in Grenada in the 1970s, I was, like others of that generation, both motivated by the Black Power movement and discussions of black politics and beginning to think of Caribbean politics in anticolonial, anti-imperialist terms. I had studied at the Mona, Jamaica campus of the University of the West Indies in the immediate aftermath of the expulsion of the Guyanese intellectual Walter Rodney and had been influenced by black political organization of the period. I was in Grenada, and participating in demonstrations, during the 1970s, when youth were actively opposing the regime of Eric Matthew Gairy. Later, I studied Latin American studies in the United States and was excited to return to Grenada to work with the Maurice Bishop government after it seized control of the country.

After the end of the revolution I felt that, in order to even begin to understand what had happened and why, I would have to go back to at least 1951, when constitutional change brought universal adult suffrage to

Grenada, and the working people and peasantry entered actively for the first time into the political life of the country.

In 1951, Eric Gairy, ex-schoolteacher and migrant worker who had just returned from Aruba, succeeded in agitating against the planter class and, as historian George Brizan puts it, 'threw the planter, local merchant, and local middle class into complete disarray'. His name – and he was popularly known as 'Uncle Gairy', a title that testifies to his paternalistic approach – 'became anathema in almost every upper- and middle-class home in Grenada' (Brizan 1984: 351). By the 1970s, however, Gairy had also managed to alienate sectors of the youth and workers.

Out of a succession of groups opposing an increasingly repressive Gairy regime during the 1970s, two, MAP (Movement for Assemblies of the People) and JEWEL (Joint Endeavour for Welfare, Education and Liberation), came together to form the New Jewel Movement (NJM), with Maurice Bishop and Unison Whiteman as Joint Coordinating Secretaries.

The NJM's flag was in African liberation colours, black, red and green. In the centre was an orange ball signifying hope. It advocated a system of people's assemblies, 'such as existed in Tanzania or Switzerland'. Its manifesto promised that, 'Besides placing power directly into the hands of the people, people's assemblies will end the divisions that the party system has brought to Grenada' (*ABC of NJM*).

Manning Marable notes that MAP's 'version of bottom-up, radical democracy drew its inspiration from C. L. R. James and from the Tanzanian model of *ujamaa vijijini*'. He adds, 'Theoretically, MAP was still quite eclectic in its political orientation. Bishop himself had a vague understanding of James's Marxism, but probably had done little serious theoretical study on his own' (Marable 1987: 208, 297). Another researcher, Anthony Thorndike (1985), analyses that although from its early days the NJM may have been broadly socialist and anti-imperialist in general outlook, it was not 'self-consciously Marxist'. In fact, the party itself stated that it was not communist, but was of the opinion 'that some of the Marxist analysis is valid ... (*ABC of NJM*).'

When the NJM emerged in Grenada, speaking of the need for a more positive self-image among the Grenadian and wider Caribbean people, I was enthusiastic. I had heard my maternal grandmother chanting stories of William the Conqueror and speaking of British history in relation to Britain's interests in 'Corsica, Sardinia, Sicily, Malta, the Lomen Islands and the islands of the archipelago in the Mediterranean'. As far as I was aware, my grandmother knew no African history and had little knowledge of the Grenadian story beyond a connection with Britain and her own close knowledge of the geography of Grenada, gained from walking its length and breadth to carry out domestic work in the houses of the (once I would have said 'wealthy'; now, understanding better the realities of the postcolonial under-classes, I say) better-off. So when a new group of young political organizers started talking about a need to revamp the education system, which was too 'colonial', I identified with it immediately.

Like Eric Gairy when he emerged, Bishop, Whiteman and other NJM organizers of the 1970s were young. In 1951, when Eric Gairy returned from working in Aruba and changed the Grenadian political landscape, he was 29 years old. Grenada was still a colony, but constitutional change had brought adult suffrage. In 1973, when Maurice Bishop became a key figure in the formation of the NJM, he, too, was 29. Grenada was on the way to being named an 'independent' nation.

The period 1974-6, the beginning of Grenada's story as an independent small state, was an important one for the NJM's development of an ideological framework. The first new party of an independent Grenada, in 1975 the NJM, apparently influenced by Bernard Coard's critique of ideological weaknesses in its anti-Gairy agitation during the 1974-5 period, decided to adopt a Marxist-Leninist vanguard structure. Coard was said to be impatient with the party's attraction to the Jamesian and Tanzanian models. In 1975, too, youth interested in discussion of Marxist theory came together to form a group called OREL (Organization for Research, Education and Liberation) and Coard became a sort of mentor to OREL. At first outside of the official NJM structure, OREL was later incorporated into the party.

Despite concerns on both sides, the New Jewel Movement and other local parties came together in an alliance for the 1976 elections, and won six seats to Gairy's nine, with the Alliance protesting that the results were inaccurate (*Torchlight* 1976, 15 December: 1). The victorious NJM candidates were Maurice Bishop, Unison Whiteman and Bernard Coard. Maurice Bishop became Leader of the Opposition and, for the next three years, the NJM continued to agitate as part of an official parliamentary opposition. Tensions between the two sides grew and eventually, on 13 March 1979, while Prime Minister Eric Gairy was away at the UN in New York, the NJM seized control of the country.

According to the NJM, it had received information that Prime Minister Gairy had left orders that NJM party members were to be killed (Ventour 2009). Reacting to this, the NJM attacked and secured the army barracks at True Blue, in the south of the island. On radio, it called on police stations to hoist a white flag indicating surrender to the new commanding forces. The NJM was so confident of popular support at this stage that it issued a call to the nation for assistance. Some two thousand people became involved in requesting the surrender of police stations (Collins 1990: 530-1). Eventually, thousands were on the streets, part of what had become a popular overthrow of the Gairy government (*Torchlight* 1976, 18 March).

This, then, was the euphoric beginning of the Grenada Revolution. The Constitution was suspended, and initially regional governments hesitated to acknowledge the new government, the first of its kind in the English-speaking Caribbean. But the regional press had for the preceding months reported the Gairy regime's brutality and popular local support gave the NJM a chance to consolidate its position.

For the four years following its seizure of government, the NJM and its People's Revolutionary Government (PRG) worked hard to improve social and economic conditions locally. I write now remembering the tremendous sense of purpose in the early days of the Grenada Revolution. People worked long hours, without expecting extra compensation. Some were party members, some not. They worked because they knew the country's story, the region's story, the story of colonial exploitation the world over, of poor economic rewards, inequality of opportunity, replication of feelings of cultural and other inferiority, exploitation of the working classes. They/we were excited about a government that knew these things too, and seemed set to change them. The PRG and the NJM talked about the American Revolution and the lessons to be learned from those early days of American anticolonial agitation. There was tremendous and infectious idealism.

Along the way, however, the NJM lost friends and supporters, increasingly becoming repressive as it tried to do social and economic work in the community with few hands and at the same time to consolidate political power without holding elections. In the 1982–3 period, tensions, apparently centring on Bishop and Coard, developed within the party. The final debacle may perhaps be most simply outlined as follows: assessing that there were weaknesses in the party structure and consequently in party effectiveness and party work, the NJM voted in 1983 for joint leadership to be shared by Maurice Bishop and Bernard Coard. Bishop, after some discussion, agreed, and voted for joint leadership. He then went on an official trip to Eastern Europe and by the time he returned had changed his mind. It was rumoured that senior party member (member of the Central Committee and Political Bureau) George Louison, who had also travelled to Eastern Europe, had a hand in Bishop's coming to that decision. Since the party had voted on the joint leadership issue, it opposed Maurice Bishop and sided with Bernard Coard, who favoured joint leadership and under whose ideological direction it was generally agreed the party worked. The party accused Bishop of 'onemanism' and not accepting the democratic centralist decision-making process. Out of this developed the perception that the Leninist vanguard was on one side and the 'hero' with his crowd, the mass of the people, on the other. Bishop was accused of starting a rumour that Coard was planning to kill him. The party put Maurice Bishop under house arrest. On the morning of 19 October, Bishop was released in a massive demonstration led by Unison Whiteman, Kenrick Radix and others. After his release, it was said that Bishop was going to address the crowds at the Market Square in the capital, St George's. However, the decision seems to have been taken to go instead to Fort Rupert. There, eventually, a confrontation between the two opposing party forces was played out. What became known as the Coard faction, opposed to the Bishop faction, sent in tanks to retake the fort. The leaders and some members of the public were assassinated, and, six days later, 25 October 1983, the US invaded.

Since the NJM was leftist and known to have Marxist-Leninist leanings, the internecine strife was a body blow to left-leaning political organizations in the region. Leftism, some argued, was to blame for Grenada's troubles, and since the faction accused of murdering Bishop was known to speak of the need for 'Leninist discipline', Leninism was also blamed. Considering this, motivated to consider if Lenin were to blame, I went to Lenin's *Left-Wing Communism: An Infantile Disorder*.[1]

Some sections of that work particularly spoke to me, but I want first to draw attention to some comments recently made by NJM Central Committee member 'Chalkie' Ventour, who was released from prison in December 2008. Quoting from a manuscript in progress written by his fellow party and Central Committee member Ewart Layne, then still in prison, Ventour read what he said were views with which he and others still in prison entirely agreed. Layne writes that he had learned

> that our world is not made up of exploiters and exploited, a lesson that our world is not made up of oppressors and oppressed, working class and capitalists. Our society is not made up of philosophical categories, our society is made up of people, of human beings. I came to realize that if one could see beyond the categories, and the formula, if one could see beyond the science, the same science which, as we often say, blinded us, if one could do this, reach out beyond the collective descriptions and reach out to the human being, then so much is possible, and I recognize in a more profound way than ever before that with all our imperfections humanity is still God's greatest creation and should so be treated. (Ventour 2009)

I quote this because even as I look at 'the science', which is how the youthful revolutionaries of the 1980s referred to their study of Marxism-Leninism, I must acknowledge that, by their own account, they are not, today, philosophically, in the place they were in 1983. They have, by their own account, learned from the years that whatever 'the book' or 'the science' might say, the study of people in their locale says more, and that seems to me a major acknowledgement of folly and fundamental error, discrediting the uncritical application of Leninism or any other philosophy.

Having recognized that acknowledgement, let us see what ideas may have affected them. This, remember, is an approach from a personal perspective, remembering the arguments of the period. According to Lenin, 'revolution is

1 The full text of *Left-Wing Communism* is online at www.archive.org/stream/leftwingcommuni00lenigoog/leftwingcommuni00lenigoog_djvu.txt.

impossible without a change in the views of the majority of the working class, and this change is brought about by the political experience of the masses, and never by propaganda alone' (Lenin 1931: 82). As I read this, it seems to me suspiciously as if Lenin and I are on the same side in this debate, that he would conclude, too, that the attitude displayed in Grenada when the faction of the party supported by the people was killed and the people alienated demonstrates 'intellectual childishness and not the serious tactics of a revolutionary class' (83).

The actions of the majority faction of the party suggest that it assessed that the *event* of 13 March, when the repressive Gairy government was toppled, had won it the revolution and so, revolution in hand, it could ignore the people and rush on to ensure consolidation of the revolutionary prize. Lenin writes:

> The Bolsheviks could not have maintained themselves in power for two and a half years, not even for two and a half months, without the most stringent, I may say iron, discipline in our party, and without the fullest and unreserved support rendered it by the working class, that is, by that part of it which is sensible, honest, devoted, influential, capable of leading, of inspiring the backward masses with enthusiasm. (Lenin 1931: 17)

'The science' seems to be saying two things here. While it advocates support from 'the whole mass of the working class', defined as its 'thinking, honest, self-sacrificing and influential elements', the Grenadian revolutionaries perhaps considered that they had already identified and secured these 'elements' within the party and so others could be ignored. But Lenin warns that with the vanguard alone, victory is impossible. It would be not only foolish, but criminal, to throw the vanguard into the final struggle so long as the whole class, the general mass, has not taken up a position either of direct support of the vanguard or at least of benevolent neutrality toward it (Lenin 1931: 92).

Indeed, reading such thoughts in *Left-Wing Communism* in the aftermath of the demise of the Grenada Revolution left me with the feeling that, despite my mistrust of the language related to the backwardness of the masses, perhaps symptomatic of my being from a small community and therefore able to put faces to those not invited to join the party or otherwise recognizable as the 'backward elements', I was, in 1983, more in agreement with Lenin than with the Grenada revolutionaries.

Some time in 1982 or 1983 one member of the NJM Central Committee asked me, 'Sister, are you a Bolshevik or a Menshevik?' Of course, one interpretation of the question is that it was simply intended as fun. That interpretation has not escaped me, though it is certainly indicative of a macabre humour, with laughter echoing right into what could perhaps be interpreted as the bullet sounds of a Grenadian Bolshevik/Menshevik split and – not the triumph of an October Revolution, but – the demise, in October 1983, of the March 1979 revolutionary beginnings.

Now, as I consider the events of October 1983, the memory of that question haunts and brings me back to consider what thoughts may have been current among the top party leadership at the time. I wonder about various sides of the Bolshevik/Menshevik argument and how it may have been seen to replicate itself in Grenada.

Briefly, the Bolshevik/Menshevik reference is to a split in the Russian Social Democratic Labour Party that began with a 1903 debate over an article. The Bolsheviks, 'the majority' eventually led by Lenin, favoured tight organization of an elite group within the party, strong central organization and the formation of a small Central Committee. They eventually led the revolution and became the Communist Party of the Soviet Union.

The 1903 Bolshevik/Menshevik argument, the beginnings of publicly expressed differences between the two groups, was at first based on dis-agreements that, some critics claim, could seem fairly minor to people outside the party. Neil Harding explains that at the 1903 Congress of the party, Lenin and Martov 'proposed differing drafts of Article 1 of the party's rules, the object of which was to define the qualifications for party membership' (Harding 1977: 190). Lenin proposed that a party member should be 'one who recognizes the party's programme and supports it by material means and by personal participation in one of the party's organizations' (Lenin in Harding 1977: 190). Martov proposed that a member be 'one who recognizes the party's programme and supports it by material means and by regular personal assistance under the direction of one of the party organizations'. Harding concludes: 'The difference between these two drafts may perhaps seem as insignificant to the contemporary reader as it did to many rather bemused delegates to the Congress, but out of such mole-hills, politics, particularly revolutionary politics, has a talent for creating great mountains' (1977: 190). In the end, the party Congress voted for Martov's version of the article and, according to Harding, Lenin thereafter set himself to ensure that what he considered a more responsible perspective be encoded by in other ways limiting party membership.

Harding's comment that 'out of such mole-hills politics ... has a talent for creating great mountains' calls to mind the Grenada situation and the reactions of non-party people to party explanations that Maurice Bishop had agreed to joint leadership and then changed his mind. While the party may have thought its explanation revealed that Bishop was unprincipled, those outside the party seemed rather bemused by the fuss over this issue. This might be simplifying matters, but what is clear is that no explanations moved people to the side of the party, and certainly not after Bishop and others were killed. In the end, the 'wrong side', it seems to me, is not the side that stood for or against joint leadership, but the side that, not having the support of the people, went ahead to try to enforce its point of view.

In the case of the Russian Democratic Party, after Martov's early victory, Lenin seems to have strategized for *his* later victory. Harding assesses that Lenin and his supporters wanted to make sure that this display of 'softness', as evidenced by the party voting for Martov's version instead of Lenin's, should be checked (Harding 1977: 191–2). After this vote, and after other decisions not acceptable to some, and the consequent departure of some of the party membership, Lenin and his group became 'the majority' or 'the Bolsheviks'. They, naturally, now pressed home their advantage to get some of their ideas recognized. Instead of a six-member Central Committee, Lenin wanted a three-man editorial board of *Iskra*, the organ of the party, and a three-man Central Committee. This would effectively be reducing Central Committee membership. Three of those previously CC members were now to be members of the editorial board of the party organ. Martov, although named as one of the members of the Central Committee, was angry at these decisions by Lenin and his supporters. Here, then, around the issue of narrowing of Central Committee membership, began the real division between Bolsheviks (the new majority voice) and the Mensheviks (the minority voice). Thinking of Grenada's majority/minority party voice split (and there was one!), I find compelling Neil Harding's analysis of the Lenin/Martov dispute: 'Issues of wounded pride immediately became inseparable from issues of principle and this was inevitable in a situation where some of the legendary heroes of the movement were being asked to withdraw from the limelight and accept a more humble role' (1977: 192).

However, while this is instructive and the Grenadian revolutionaries could have learned from the experiences of comrades in the Soviet Union or elsewhere, I still assess that the major problem may have been that, for Grenada, the Soviet experience became the main text and not just a supportive script.

I remember the tone of the question asked of me, the slight smile, the waiting – a watching: 'Are you a Bolshevik or a Menshevik?' Now, in retrospect, I conclude that the question was asked at a time when there was in the party a perception of 'Bolshevik' and 'Menshevik' camps, and the concept of 'Bolshevik' meant only 'majority' of an elite vanguard party and the people were entirely forgotten. The question was, in fact, the ultimate evidence of the party's narcissism.

The Grenadian people were not generally Marxist-Leninist or even knowingly capitalist in orientation. They were working out of their own critique of existence, their perceptions of practical, personal experience. To quote one woman's comment from the early days of the Grenada Revolution, 'If what going on here is communism, well, it look OK'. It seems to me that those attracted to the idea of a Leninist vanguard began to label all meaningful activity Leninist, and to, in practice, devalue the role of local history and practical experience, perhaps even to be attracted to Stalinist rhetoric without naming it.

As I read Lenin, I note his review of the British situation, the German situation, the Russian situation. I wonder if we, working for Grenada, had forgotten the particular history of Grenada and the Caribbean. In the minds of the main political actors of the time, Grenada's story – a story of Amerindian, African, Indian, some poor European people and the various mixtures in the blood of that coming together – was no longer of preponderant importance. A 13 October 1983 resolution of the armed forces branch of the NJM, clearly written at the height of the crisis, noted:

> Never would we allow cultism, egoism, the unreasonable and unprincipled desires of one man or a minority to be imposed on our party thus stiffling [sic] inner party democracy and endangering the party and revolution and holding our country to ransom. We demand an immediate end to this and the restoration of Leninist norms of party life and their strict observance by all as the key for the normal functioning of the party.[2]

2 The resolution appears online at www.thegrenada revolutiononline. com/praresolution. html, copyright 2001–2009, Ann Elizabeth Wilder. It is also listed in the Grenada Documents Collection, Folder Register, Georgetown University Libraries, online at www.library. georgetown.edu/ dept/speccoll/ grenreg.htm (Box 2, Folder 4, Resolution of PRA – October 12, 1983. Date span: 12 October 1983. Description: Resolution of the People's Revolutionary Army supporting the Central Committee and joint leadership of the party/PRG).

Stuck in the well of democratic centralism, and forgetting all else, there was no way for either side to climb out. Principle ruled.

I remember another moment – Foreign Minister Unison Whiteman, later killed at the fort, telling me, just before the events of 19 October, that OREL had its own intentions within the party and that, now, it was 'civil war'. On both sides, egos were hurt, there was mutual disappointment, and there was no way back, it seems, to remembering the people who depended so much on the good sense of their leaders.

In *Caribbean Revolutions and Revolutionary Theory* (1993), Brian Meeks offers what I think is a useful analysis of how the 1983 situation developed. He avoids conspiracy theories and looks at the organic development of OREL, first as a group of high school students coming together to discuss shared interest in Marxism-Leninism and then a group further motivated by Bernard Coard in 1976. He sees them not as a sleeping cell waiting to wreak havoc, but as a group of friends with similar ideas, who might, I conclude, well come together for discussion. Bishop and Coard, Meeks also concludes, had different responsibilities in the party. Bishop gradually emerged as the 'hero'-type leader, a circumstance facilitated by the party, even though it may have later come to resent that.

Even this has to be analysed within the context of postcolonial politics. What patterns of political leadership had existed in Grenada? What, consciously or not, did the NJM itself promote as it tried to consolidate power? Was the party membership more influenced by the autocratic patterns of colonial rule than it acknowledged or even realized? How could vanguard politics and the personality of the 'hero' leader be reconciled? It seems that in the end the party decided to use colonial high-handedness, or Gairyite repressiveness, and labelled it all Leninist discipline. One wonders if it is ever 'the book' that matters. One could put a hand on the Bible and justify slavery, or on Lenin's collected works and justify repression.

Several questions remain for me. If my revolutionary friends had known less about Leninism and more about Grenadian history and society, would they still be leading the Grenada Revolution today? If they had known *more* about Leninism, would they be leading the Grenada Revolution today? As I listen to 'Chalkie' Ventour, I ask what is perhaps the question that looks to the future, as a lesson for present and future leaders: had they been more mature, more informed, less overworked and more able to give calm assessment to the alternatives, would they be leading the Grenada Revolution today?

References

Brizan, G. (1984) *Grenada, Island of Conflict: From Amerindians to People's Revolution 1498–1979*, London: Zed Books.

Collins, M. (1990) 'Grenada: a political history 1950–1979.' Ph.D. thesis, London School of Economics.

Harding, N. (1977) *Lenin's Political Thought: Theory and Practice in the Democratic Revolution, Volume 1*, New York: St Martin's Press.

Lenin, V. I. (1931) [1920] *Left-Wing Communism, An Infantile Disorder*, Detroit: Marxian Educational Society.

Marable, M. (1987) *African and Caribbean Politics*, London: Verso.

Meeks, B. (1993) *Caribbean Revolutions and Revolutionary Theory*, London: Macmillan Caribbean.

The New Jewel (n.d.) *The ABC of NJM. Questions and Answers on NJM – its History, Ideas, Principles*. Grenada: NJM.

Thorndike, A. (1985) *Grenada: Politics, Economics and Society*, London: Frances Pinter.

Ventour, J. 'Chalkie' (2009) MTV interview by Josephine 'Jojo' McGuire, 3 June.

THE CUBAN REVOLUTION AND THE CARIBBEAN

Civil Society, Culture and International Relations

Rafael Hernández

Editor, Revista Tema

Cuba has historically interacted with a variety of regional actors and powers, both Caribbean and American. Political links with revolutionaries throughout the Caribbean before 1959 influenced Cuba's susbequent role in the region. The postcolonial Caribbean and Cuba developed a synergic relationship, although not one without contradictions. The Grenadian and the Sandinista revolutions renovated Cuban ideology, diminishing the influence of Soviet Marxism and atheism. The tragic end of the Grenadian Revolution contributed to the process of rectifying Cuban errors initiated in 1985, and was a main factor in a new Cuban strategic defensive system which was based not on the supposed alliance with the USSR but on territorial militias. Cuban wars in Southwest Africa in the 1970s and 1980s deepened Cuba's ties and prestige within the Caribbean. In the post-Cold War era, cooperation and diplomatic relations strengthened these ties, creating a new political environment within the region. Beyond trade and tourism, Cuba and the Caribbean share a common interest in areas such as education, public health, social policy, fighting drug traffic, civilian defence against hurricanes, national and public security, and protection of cultural industries and the environment. Improved relations between the US and Cuba would benefit the whole Caribbean region.

In a recess during the meetings that took place under the direction of the Ministry of the Revolutionary Armed Forces (MINFAR) to analyse the Grenada events after the US invasion of 1983, the Army General Raúl Castro, minister of the armed forces, withdrew from the room. Upon reinitiating the session, Raúl appeared, dressed in a *guayabera* instead of the olive green uniform of the Cuban military. Addressing the auditorium of high officials convened in the Sierra Maestra building, he declared that as of that moment he was not going to speak as the minister of the armed forces, but rather as the second secretary of the party. His speech that day severely criticized the Cuban armed forces, the ministry of the interior and the party for the actions that had led to the overthrow of the Grenadian government and the intervention of the United States, which, in a combat in which North American troops and Cuban forces came face to face for the first time, had resulted in the death of a group of Cuban civil workers in Grenada.

Other subsequent events also illustrate how the military in its multiple roles inside and outside of Cuba has been subject to scrutiny and subordinated to the authority of the government and the party. The most important such events were the 1989 public judicial proceedings against high officials of the ministry of the armed forces and the ministry of the interior, accused of business dealings with narcotrafficking networks in the Caribbean basin, and of acts of corruption, abuse of power, and fraudulent operations, placing national security at risk (Martí 1989).

In both cases, it was reaffirmed that the condition of being in the military or being a high official did not create immunity before the law, nor did it justify any action that implied deposing the defence before other interests or exposing the mechanisms of national security. This was a critical moment in the Cuban revolutionary process, one of several periodic reevaluations that have characterized the Cuban revolutionary process and reaffirmed the need to continually reexamine the concentration of political power and its charges (Escalante 2008). The fall of the Grenada Revolution and the US invasion of Grenada in 1983 and the fall of the Soviet Union in 1989 were two occasions for such adjustments, which were critical for the survival of the Cuban Revolution.

This essay considers the significance that the relationships with the Greater Caribbean have had not only for Cuban politics and national security, but also for political culture, for Cuban perceptions about themselves and about the outside world, and for the series of ideological transitions that have been experimented with on the island throughout the revolutionary period.

Cuban-Caribbean Relations and the Border Condition

The national shield of Cuba suggests the destiny of the island: between two tips of land, one golden key on a rising sun. Cuba, flanked by the Yucatan and Florida peninsulas, projects a silhouette of a key that opens the path to the West Indies upon a dawn of liberty. That geostrategic location has presided over Cuban history since colonial times. Without precious mineral deposits nor other natural riches that motivated the colonizers, Cuba started as a base for the expeditions that conquered Mexico and Florida for the Spanish Crown in the sixteenth century; to rapidly be converted into a crossroads of paths of the New World, naval station and interoceanic place of trade, object of British desire that, from its nearby colony of Jamaica, could go so far as overtake Havana in the middle of the eighteenth century, or a site of immediate refuge for the French planters of Saint Domingue, who escaped from the Haitian Revolution, until the end of the eighteenth century. Its proximity enabled Southern slaves to imagine Cuba as one more star in the North American Union in the nineteenth century; and led Alfred T. Mahan in the beginning of the twentieth century to conceive of Cuba as the pontoon to dominate the quadrilateral region of the Caribbean, with New Orleans, Trinidad and Cartagena of the Indies (Mahan 1899).

On the other hand, the North American border of the island, dominated by the United States, has given way to a special North American gravitation towards politics and Cuban society throughout the two centuries (Guerra 1935; Portell Vilá 1941; Roig de Leuchsenring 1923; Pérez 1988). Indeed, the annexing currents, the impacts of the civil war, the power of J. P. Morgan and the beet growers in Washington, the resolutions and laws of the North American Congress regarding the desired political regime on the island, the activity of the Cuban emigrants in the USA since the war of 1868, or the desires and determinations of Thomas Jefferson, James Polk, John Quincy Adams, William MacKinley, Teddy and Franklin Roosevelt, Dwight Eisenhower – to mention only those presidents before 1959 – have constituted events and actors in the history of Cuba. It is not strange that the current Cuban flag has been designed in that Caribbean city called New Orleans; and that from that city an armed expedition was initiated for the first time, financed by Louisiana slave planters, in a revolution against Spain. In fact, all of these acts and characters in the history of the United States early converted Cuba in the southern flank of North America – in other words, in her *third* border.

Without the Caribbean border, it is impossible to understand Cuban history, including the most recent. Even though the English never could take over the island, the vast expansive cycle of the Cuban sugar economy in the first third of the twentieth century was possible due to the thousands of sugar cane cutters that emigrated to Cuba, from Jamaica and the Virgin Islands as far as St Kitts and Barbados, and settled down especially in the oriental provinces. Even though there was never another revolution in the Caribbean like the Haitian Revolution, the peasants of that country were those who carried the weight of the coffee boom in the Sierra Maestra mountains since the beginning of the nineteenth century. Even though none of them were recognized by official history, their surnames – Stevenson, Lafitta, Duverger – can be found amid the champions of boxing and the most famous baseball players. Their religions – especially Haitian Vodou – are still respected and practised in regions of Cuba like Santiago de Cuba or Guantanamo. Their rhythms, especially reggae, have been recognized, absorbed and assimilated by the most powerfully expressive artistic manifestations of Cuban culture and insignia of its national identity, popular dancing music.

Cuban Internationalism and Its Impact on Caribbean Revolutionary Movements

1 This nationalist project achieved its most articulated expression in the Cuban Constitution of 1940 and expressed itself in the activism of international Cuban politics advocated by the governments of the Authentic Cuban Revolutionary Party (1944–52), especially in international bodies like the UN and the OAS.

There already existed several projects for anticolonial or anti-capitalist national sovereignty in pre-revolutionary Cuba.[1] Comparable movements in the history of the greater Caribbean would find support from the revolution that seized power in 1959. Indeed, the international system moulded by the Cold War and by processes of rupture and postcolonial transition in the Third World – especially in Africa, Asia and, in some ways, the Caribbean – transfigured the world, and created new real and virtual spaces for Cuba.

Since the colonial era, geographic contiguity has decisively influenced Cuban involvement with the countries inside the Great Caribbean line. Indeed, developments in the Dominican Republic, Puerto Rico, Guatemala, Nicaragua, Panama, Mexico and Venezuela are inescapable in Cuban narrative since the nineteenth century (Franco 1961, 1965). In the first half of the twentieth century, Cuba was a refuge for political exiles who fought against the dictatorships of Juan Vicente Gómez (Venezuela), Anastasio Somoza (Nicaragua) and Rafael Leónidas Trujillo (Dominican Republic) that, like before, a large number of Caribbean combatants had incorporated into the ranks of the Liberation Army during the wars of independence. It is not strange, then, that well before the Cuban Revolution, expedition members of a large part of the Antilles left to fight in support of the government of Jacobo Arbenz in Guatemala (1954) and against the Dominican dictatorship (1947). The experience of international solidarity and active participation of the Caribbean revolutionaries was thus neither an initiative of the Komintern nor of the communist parties in the basin. Thousands of combatants from diverse ideological backgrounds came

2 On 16 December 1947, the Caribbean Pact was signed in Guatemala, under the auspices of President Juan José Arévalo, who acted as arbiter. Its signatories were Juan Rodríguez García, 'on behalf of the peoples of Santo Domingo', José Figueres, on behalf of Costa Rica, and Emiliano Chamorro, Gustavo Manzanares, Pedro José Zepeda and Rosendo Argüello, on behalf of Nicaragua. Its purpose was 'to continue to overthrow each one of the three dictatorships that we intend to combat', forming for it 'one sole revolutionary team, with all the economic, war and human resources that we are capable of providing' in order to establish constitutional order, justice and

together in the Abraham Lincoln brigade for the defence of the Spanish Republic (1936–9). It was the Caribbean Legion (1946–50), founded by various political and military figures of the basin,[2] that incited the overthrow of the Trujillo dictatorship, by means of the frustrated expedition of Cayo Confites, with the participation of numerous Caribbean combatants – among them, the young lawyer Fidel Castro and General Alberto Bayo, who would later train the Granma yacht expedition members. From the Costa Rican capital, José Figueres (one of the leaders of the Legion) then organized military expeditions to overthrow the regimes of Nicaragua and the Dominican Republic.

Thus, when the small column of combatants directed by the Cuban commander Delio Gómez Ochoa disembarked in Quisqueya on 14 June 1959, a few days before the victory of the revolution, it was not doing anything essentially original, nor was it frowned upon, not even by social democratic leaders like José Figueres, Rómulo Betancourt or Luis Muñoz Marín. Rather, it was continuing an already established practice in Caribbean political culture, albeit one reinforced by the extraordinary victory over the Batista dictatorship. Those who fought against a dictatorship – whether in Haiti, El Salvador or Colombia – did not need to subscribe to a Marxist ideology or belong to the Communist Party to share a revolutionary identity.

It is such a cultural-political identity that operates in the internationalist impulse of the Cuban Revolution towards the Greater Caribbean. This identity has been nourished by foreign combatants who participated in Cuba's own civil war: those, starting with Che Guevara, who arrived in the first hours of victory to give their support to the incipient revolutionary process. As in past decades, Havana was once again converted into a place of exile and conspiracy of revolutionaries of the region – this time with the powerful support of a state that wanted 'to make the revolution'.

The Impact of the Caribbean on the Cuban Revolution (1959–2009)

democracy. (José del Castillo, 'Legión del Caribe, una multinacional revolucionaria', online at DiarioLibre.com.)

Caribbean space has been a significant theme in Cuban diplomacy since the revolution, for the English Caribbean islands became independent at about the same time that the Cuban Revolution triumphed. Moreover, Jamaica, Guyana, Trinidad and Tobago, and Barbados established relations with Cuba in 1972, positioning themselves among the first countries that initiated the thawing of relations with the Cuban Revolution in the hemisphere. Headed by leaders as ideologically diverse as Forbes Burnham, Cheddi Jaggan, Michael Manley and Eric Williams, this thawing provided an incentive to the recovery of Caribbean ties that, in the end, turned out to be more lasting than other Cuban alliances. Although the Cuban Revolution is often thought of in terms of its alliances with the USSR and Eastern Europe, its sense of belonging – its mark of origin, one could say – remained on the side of the Caribbean and Latin American revolutions. Beginning in 1970–2, Cuba's reconnection with the region by means of consecutive diplomatic restorations that led to the lifting of the isolation agreement in the OAS in 1975,[3] would give way to an international reinsertion that, like in the years before the 1990s, would influence the Cuban domestic context. This reinsertion not only brought the theme of strategic alliances and political realism out into the open, but also demonstrated a genuine willingness to have dialogue and a more plural space for ideological exchange. The 'brother countries' were now not limited to the 'popular democracies' of Eastern Europe, but extended to all those countries, especially in the Third World, that took on respectful coexistence and constructive dialogue with the Cuban Revolution.

The peak of the Third World phenomenon since the 1970s also represented an ideological opening in Marxist-Leninist orthodoxy. Thus, Cuban relations with the non-aligned movement and in particular with Africa, facilitated an international space amenable to meeting with non-communist leaders like Manley, Williams, Khadafi, Machel and Nyerere. The Cuban-African-Caribbean triangle wove a new web of interests, rooted in common political cultures, unconnected to sectarianism and hegemony. Caribbean support for Cuban solidarity in the Angolan war (1975) led a government so ideologically different from Cuba – Barbados – to permit technical stopovers of military flights from Cuba bound for the African battleground. Ever since then, this link with Africa has been part of a common feeling that has facilitated dialogue between Cuba and its neighbours, especially the Eastern Caribbean, and part of an interweaving that goes beyond high commissions and embassies to include popular consensus.

Another of the significant effects of the Caribbean on the Cuban revolutionary process was the reorientation of Cuba's religious politics. Indeed, the primary factors that changed the tide between church and state in Cuba *came from* the Caribbean. If, indeed, the strategic encounter between Christians and Marxists that took place in Allende's Chile was a first step towards a comparable thawing in Cuba, it was not until the visit of Fidel, the leader of the revolution, and his dialogue with the Jamaican Council of Churches of that country that a tendency to change was initiated, permanently driven by two big subsequent events. The first was the Conference of Catholic Bishops of Puebla (1979), which fostered a spirit of dialogue within the Catholic Church and made room for a decisive event: the First National Ecclesiastical Meeting (ENEC) held in Cuba that same year. The second, which had a notable effect upon Cuban domestic religious

3 The consent that permitted the Inter-American system to impose total breakage with the island beginning with the Cuban missile crisis (1962), and that closed completely in 1965, would start to change in 1970–4. Panama, Colombia, Venezuela and other countries in the region, like Peru and Argentina, would regain their connections with Cuba in the middle of the 1970s.

politics, was the Sandinista Revolution. Prestigious religious figures of Sandinismo like Chancellor Miguel D'Escoto, Minister for Culture Ernesto Cardenal, and his brother Fernando, also a priest, used to visit Cuba and maintained close relationships with Cuban Catholic intellectuals who had been relegated to the background in 1971–6. This was the case for Cintio Vitier, Eliseo Diego, Fina García Marruz and others. The Cubans working in Nicaragua in fields such as culture, sports and education had to overcome the prejudices and practices of atheist Marxism taught in Cuba in those years. The idea of a place for Christian thought inside revolutionary ideology, particularly liberation theology, was gaining followers in Cuba itself.

Although not exempt from contradictions, an easing of tensions between church and state began in Cuba; it gave support to the restoration of churches and the disposition of means by the churches in Cuba. In fact, it slowly began to undermine atheism as a necessary ingredient of Cuban Marxism. If the destiny of the Cuban Revolution was united with all of the other revolutions in Africa and Latin America, and especially the Caribbean, it became clear that these were not going to be directed by a simple 'tactical' or 'strategic alliance' between Christians and Marxists, but rather simply by revolutionaries whose religious creeds did not matter. The parallel experiences of the insurgencies in El Salvador and Guatemala throughout the 1980s would reinforce this approach. These events did not result in merely cosmetic or diplomatic changes to Cuban revolutionary discourse, nor were they matters of convenience. Rather, these were experiences that saturated Cuban society itself. The thousands of educators, doctors, experts and military advisers who collaborated in the Sandinista Revolution, like the tens of thousands who participated in the political processes in the Southeast and in the Horn of Africa in those same years, would experience them directly.

Transitions in Cuban-Caribbean Relations: Values, Crisis and Continuity

The revolution led by the New Jewel in Grenada (1979–83) had a deep impact on political processes, civic culture and Cuban revolutionary ideology. Maurice Bishop quickly became a popular figure on the island thanks to his youth, charisma, style and revolutionary 'outside-the-box' discourse. But above all, Grenada, like the Sandinista Revolution, was seen as partly enabled by the struggles undertaken by Cuba, which gave impetus to the revolutions in Latin America and the Caribbean since the 1960s. Soviet politics toward the Third World, its interpretations of Latin American reality through the lens of the Communist parties of the region, and the manuals of Soviet Marxism-Leninism that were used inside Cuba, did not have much to do with the Sandinista movement and the revolutionary ideologies in the Caribbean. In fact, the revolutions in the Caribbean worked against the grain of that discourse, including its anti-religious component.

On the other hand, Cuba, in its relationship with Grenada, played the unusual role of the 'big country'. The larger island in effect played a role as advocate of the Grenadian and Nicaraguan revolutions to the USSR and the socialist camp. The Cuban leadership translated the ideologies of the Sandinista movement and the New Jewel into the codes of the Eurasian communist parties in an effort to secure financial support and favourable trade terms for Grenada and Nicaragua. From their own experiences, Cuban leaders were aware of the social erosion and narrowing of political choices that economic strangulation could exert upon society, and so, in an apparent paradox, Fidel Castro did not advise radicalism to these young revolutionaries, but rather moderation.

The presence of not only military advisers, but also Cuban contractors and health workers in Grenada at the juncture of the North American invasion, embodied this approach. However, Cubans – solidarity workers and the government – were far from imagining that Grenada would be the stage upon which Cuban and North American military forces would confront each other for the first time. This event caused deep shock in Cuba. The failure to foresee the internal political crisis in the Grenadian leadership, as well as the mistakes made in the confrontation leading to the invasion, had the bitter outcome of a military defeat for Cuba, and dealt a strong political and moral blow to the institutions of the revolution and Cuban society.

This impact and the self-criticizing exercise that accompanied it served as a preamble to the process of rectifying errors and negative tendencies that the Cuban party would initiate two years later, in 1985. Among the changes were the revision of responsibilities in the party, the ministry of the revolutionary armed forces (MINFAR) and the Cuban ministry of the interior (MININT). As part of this process, and in the face of open threats by the Reagan administration, the Cuban strategic defensive stance would transform into a 'War of All the People' (*Guerra de Todo el Pueblo*), developing a system of defence based solely on Cuba's own resources and on the decentralization of the war theatre, and not on an alliance with the USSR and Soviet military strategy. The collapse of the Grenadian Revolution, and the unequal military confrontation between Cubans and North Americans which ensued, made the role of the territorial militias a central strategy of resistance to a foreign invader.

Throughout the second half of the 1980s, this process would create a deeper and more democratic critical revision than would have occurred in the Cuban Revolution *since then*, culminating in the broad popular discussion of the Appeal of the IV Congress of the Cuban Communist Party (PCC) in 1990. This public debate interrogated the institutional model of

Cuban socialism established in 1976, its practices, style and modes of thinking, including those inspired by the USSR and Eastern Europe. In fact, this resulted in the most important precedent of the critical debates on the deficiencies of the socialist model, which Raúl Castro would convene in July 2007.

The crisis unleashed by the combined effect of the exhaustion of that model and the end of the socialist bloc led to an abrupt rupture in the international system, which would represent a challenge for revolutionary politics. The 'Special Period', as it was called, would inaugurate a qualitatively distinct phase in foreign relations, characterized not only by an accentuated activism, but also by meta-diplomacy.

Lacking an alliance with any bloc or superpower, facing a drastically reduced military capacity as a result of the end of the conflict in Southeast Africa, immersed in a profound decline in economic growth, the Cuban government staked its most valuable resource – human capital – in a new politics of which the spearhead was civil cooperation. The theatre *par excellence* for those politics was the Caribbean and Africa. Doctors, teachers, sports trainers and art instructors deployed in this cooperation reached places that diplomats had never reached on the island. After having invested fifteen years in military operations for the defence of Angola and the independence of Namibia, and having assisted the Sandinistas for over a decade, and when it seemed that Cuban internationalism was already history, these new projects of cooperation took young Cuban professionals to places like Guatemala, Haiti, Paraguay and Honduras, where Cubans had not set foot since 1959; and to other places where they had never been and to where it seemed they would never be able to return, like Grenada; and to almost all of the small states in the Caribbean.

Indeed, today, Cuba maintains diplomatic, commercial and cooperative links with an increasing number of governments in the hemisphere. Besides Venezuela, Bolivia, Ecuador and Nicaragua, its relations with Brazil, Argentina, Panama and even Chile – with all of the Caribbean and almost all of Central America – are better than ever. In the diplomatic field alone, these amount to 181 countries, which span all of Latin America and the Caribbean – including the recent decision of the Arias government of Costa Rica and the reestablishment that is expected upon the triumph of the central-leftist coalition in El Salvador.[4] Cubans have not felt so accompanied and diplomatically recognized in all of their history, for these relations include China and Russia, together with allies of the United States like Canada and the European Union.

4 Of the 192 member nations of the UN, Cuba has a direct presence in 120 of them with embassies; 103 of them have accredited embassies in Havana. See the intervention of the Cuban ambassador in the conference 'The Normalization of Cuban-European Union relations and the Potential for Development Cooperation', online at www.america. cubaminrex.cu/ Actualidad/2008/ Mayo/ Intervencion.html.

Cuba, the Caribbean and the Other Frontier

With the US presidential elections barely over, the prime minister of Antigua and Barbuda and president *pro tempore* of the Caribbean Community (CARICOM), Baldwin Spencer, urged Barack Obama to change US policies on the trade embargo on Cuba. This news only confirmed the politics of the Caribbean countries since the 1970s. However, its importance exceeds that of mere diplomatic declaration.

The future dynamics of these relations promise to become more complex yet. The combination of domestic factors in the United States and Cuba with regional and global factors exceeds the contingency of a new president, as exceptional as he may be. For never in the last half-century has the island – its leadership, but also its society and political culture – been so exposed to the outside world. More than 2 million tourists visited Cuba in 2006, a presence whose effect would be difficult to exaggerate. That which converts Cuba into a tourist magnet is not, obviously, solely the beaches and sunshine, nor its diversity and patrimony, but rather its culture, educated workforce and low crime rate. Nor should one underestimate the interest that is aroused in tourists by Cuba's political system and its recent history – in part precisely because of its controversial nature.

Within this context, what can Cuba expect from an increasingly porous border with the United States? What can Cuba offer to the Caribbean besides its experience in managing education, public health and other themes of social politics? If one thing it shares with the Caribbean are hurricanes, the developed capacity for confronting natural disasters could be a good example of transferable experience, not only toward the rest of the Caribbean, but also toward the United States. Cuban citizens acquire through military service, the territorial troops of the militia and the civil defence not only the capability to confront a military attack, but also fundamental skills like practice in organization and mobilization in order to confront anything from hurricanes to epidemics. This means that the responsibilities of national and public security are not concentrated in the hands of the armed forces, but rather divided between diverse institutions and levels of civil society.

The development of civic culture also runs parallel to the possibility of organized responses to such challenges to social stability and public order as narcotrafficking and illegal emigration. In Cuba, this system involves not only the armed forces and its experts in civil defence, but all scientific institutions, the media, social organizations and the population in general.

Such capabilities could contribute to a common acceptance by the Caribbean and the United States of an agenda dealing with problems that affect everyone. If indeed Cuban relations with the United States have not changed on an intergovernmental level, then they have changed with other North American actors within the political system and civil society. At least since 1995, both government and society on the island have had increased interaction with these non-governmental North American actors on a scale unknown since 1959. The 1993–5 reforms in Cuba aroused the interest of North American businesses. The 1995–6 Migration Accord was a sign of rationality from the USA that raised hopes. Despite the signing of the Helms-Burton Law (1996), academic, religious, scientific and cultural institutions on both sides increased their contacts using channels marginal to political institutions. The Cuban government declared that it was in favour of these exchanges. Other subsequent events like the Elian González case, the success of the documentary *Buena Vista Social Club*, and the visit of Pope John Paul II to Havana (1998, 1999) drew North American public attention to the human and social dimension of these exchanges. Despite resistances and adverse factors on both sides, this dialogue could be extended with active participation from the rest of the Caribbean in years to come.

Translated by Brooke Hammond-Pérez, Carlos Cañuelas and Shalini Puri

References

Escalante, General de División (r) Fabián (2008) 'Entrevista sobre la confrontación política fue en todas partes', Rafael Hernández, *Temas* 56 (October-December).

Franco, J. L. (1961) *Relaciones de Cuba y México durante el período colonial*, Havana: Instituto de Historia, Academia de Ciencias.

Franco, J. L. (1965) *Revoluciones y conflictos internacionales en el Caribe*, Havana: Instituto de Historia, Academia de Ciencias.

Guerra, R. (1935) *La expansión territorial de los Estados Unidos a expensas de España y de los países hispanoamericanos*, Havana: Cultural.

Mahan, A. T. (1899) 'The relations of the United States to their new dependencies', *Engineering Magazine (January)* in *Lessons of the War with Spain and Other Articles*, New York: Little, Brown.

Martí, J. (ed.) (1989) *Causa Uno: Fin de la conexión cubana*. Havana.

Pérez, L. A. (1988) *Cuba and the United States: Ties of Singular Intimacy*, Athens: University of Georgia Press.

Portell Vilá, H. (1941) *Historia de Cuba en sus relaciones con los Estados Unidos y España*, Havana: Jesús Montero.

Roig de Leuchsenring, E. (1923) *Análisis de las consecuencias de la intervención norteamericana en los asuntos internos de Cuba*, Havana: Imprenta El Siglo XX.

THE CONTENT OF SOCIALISM IN CUBA TODAY

Rafael Rojas

Center for Economic Research and Teaching, Mexico

This essay explores the contradictory and unstable genealogies of the concept of socialism in Cuba. It argues against the socialism practised by the single-party Cuban state, and points out that alternative, critical socialisms are not viable in Cuba today, since the state remains the final arbiter of culture and determines the terms of cultural debate.

What do intellectual elites and politicians from Havana understand by *socialism*? We can better understand its socialization if we separate this word from two other concepts, *revolution* and *fatherland*. As with any name of a regime, socialism implies loyalty to its leaders, subjects and memories implicated in the preservation of a political legacy; consent of the governed; and the whole repertoire of egalitarian and nationalistic values. Ideologically, being socialist means believing in the 'superiority' of the system, in contrast to its opposites, capitalism and democracy, especially in the matter of social justice. This sentimental and ideological combination, however, is not able to convey the significance of the concept, called for in 1979 by Cornelius Castoriadis (1992).

We are speaking here of the ideological and political content of the concept of socialism and not of socialism understood as *time,* or as a synonym for the historic period of the revolution. Seen as a word that designates the period 1959–2009 in the history of Cuba, the concept persists in the fallacy that since the revolution ruptured the previous political regime (the republic of 1902–58) and transformed society from a position of power, the revolution still exists and, in fact, is eternal. One can refer to this socialism, assumed as an indefinite time or as the state, in J. M. Coetzee's words regarding the Hobbesian citizen who is born and dies as a subject of a legal and political entity which transcends the realm of his rights and duties:

> Every account of the origins of the state starts from the premise that 'we' – not 'we' the readers but some generic 'we' so wide as to exclude no one – participate in its coming into being. But the fact is that the only 'we' we know – ourselves and the people close to us – are born into the state; and our forebears too were born into the state as far back as we can trace. The state is always there before we are. (Coetzee 2008: 11)

Following the premise of historic eternity, the Cuban Constitution of 1992, reformed in 2002, establishes that 'socialism is irrevocable', although it never specifies what socialism is. Due to the constitutional structure of the regime, socialism could mean a single party, a statist economy, and the ideology of Marx, Lenin and Martí.

But this description of the regime does not exhaust the significance of the concept either, since hypothetically there could be socialists who agree with a certain degree of privatization of the economy or who profess a type of Marxism different from that which the Constitution vaguely establishes. Thus, we will have to break down the term with greater subtlety.

In the tradition of the Marxist Left, we can detect at least three meanings of socialism:

1   The socialism of social democracy, which permits the market, representative government, and freedom of association and expression. This socialism extends from Karl Kautsky to Anthony Giddens and identifies the European social democrats, the British labourites and (rhetoric and solidarities apart) many North American liberals.

2   Soviet or totalitarian socialism, which maintains a single party and a statist economy, and which is understood as a 'transitional period' to communism. This includes the socialisms of Lenin, Stalin and Mao which, with different nuances, characterized the Soviet Union and the Eastern European regimes until 1989.

3   Radical or 'democratic' socialism, defended historically by anarchists, Trotskyites, Gramscians and any number of contemporary neo-Marxist movements. This last type of socialism does not always accept the market, but opposes state control and defends public freedoms, even if their most extreme versions endorse anti-globalization or subaltern authoritarianism. In contrast to the first two senses of socialism, this third one lacks concrete political experience, and is best understood as a theoretical gesture of the anti-Stalinist Left which in the last decades of the twentieth century resulted in the late Frankfurt School and a good part of postmodern thought: Anderson, Jameson, Eagleton, Bourdieu, Derrida, Laclau, Mouffe, Vattimo, Sloterdijk, Žižek, Badiou and many others.

Peter Sloterdijk presents the ideological tension between social democracy and communism as the dichotomy between an 'earthly' and 'celestial' Left. The former moves within a Bismarckian logic in which politics is no more than the art of the possible. The latter aspires to the '*affaire* with the infinite', conscious that it is 'characteristic of the great culture in that it favours the implantation of the impossible in the real' (Sloterdijk 2005: 310–12). However, Sloterdijk understands that communist utopia is indissoluble from an earthly, pragmatic dimension, through which 'abstract universalism' becomes a 'treacherous extravagance'. From this he concludes: 'The politicians of totalitarian conceptions of the twentieth century have demonstrated how far they can take, in so few years, the seizure of power of ghostly programmes at the cost of the forces of immunity based on the *polis* of the local civil spirits' (311).

Cuban socialism corresponds to this type of communism. Its position would be more to the left of social democracy and more to the right of neo-Marxism, although, as we shall see, this location does not mean that it occupies any kind of centre, but rather that, strictly speaking, it is out of place. The official Cuban ideology, which historically has lacked a theoretical vocation, has to do some symbolic juggling to legitimize a totalitarian order in the midst of the twenty-first century. This ideology, as Terry Eagleton suggests, would emerge not from some sound theoretical essay on the topic, but rather from the laws and institutions of the regime, and in the vision of society and the state held by the leaders of the Communist Party of Cuba: Raúl Castro, José Ramón Machado Ventura, José Ramón Balaguer and Esteban Lazo.

Cuba shares a phenomenon with all of the Latin American Left: the theoretical precariousness of its political projects. Thirty or forty years ago, Latin American socialists were reading Sartre, Althusser, Gramsci or Marcuse seriously. However, since the 1980s, intellectuals have migrated from the parties and organizations of the Left to academia, literature or journalism, which has left the professional politicians without theory. The place that theory used to occupy is occupied today by the mass media of new democracies. Hence, the ideology of Latin American leftist governments does not extend beyond philosophical packaging or historically untenable mixtures.

Let us look at two of these displacements in Cuban ideology in the last couple of decades. In 1992, when the Soviet Union disappeared, the intellectual and political elites of the island broke with Soviet Marxism, which they had endorsed for over thirty years, and adopted a post-Marxist nationalism with two primordial sources: Martí's revolutionary politics and a germinal Catholicism. In the 1990s, a nationalist identitarian discourse (Armando Hart, Cintio Vitier, Eusebio Leal, Abel Prieto, Eliades Acosta, Enrique Ubieta, etc.) became hegemonic under the legitimizing apparatus of the regime. The first phase of the so called 'battle of ideas' at the end of that decade was armed with this discourse and one of its principal architects, Eliades Acosta, came to be the cultural secretary of the Communist Party of Cuba.

At the beginning of the 1990s, Catholic nationalism showed signs of exhaustion, and the official ideology began carefully to shift towards the 'socialism of the twenty-first century' proposed by Hugo Chávez in Venezuela. Some Guevarian intellectuals of the generation of *Pensamiento Crítico*, such as Fernando Martínez Heredia, Juan Valdés Paz, Germán Sánchez and Aurelio Alonso, repositioned themselves along the lines of Chávez, and various Cuban cultural institutions such as Casa de las Américas or the Instituto Cubano del Libro became deeply involved in the aforementioned platform. However, the Communist Party of Cuba has not fully endorsed the socialist doctrine of the twenty-first century.

Chávez's doctrine fuses Marx and Bolívar, a fusion which comes undone in Marx's 1858 essay, 'Bolívar and Ponte', written under the charge of Charles Dana for *The New American Cyclopaedia*. Looking at this text by Marx, only two reactions exist: one either thinks that Marx was a Eurocentric racist who did not understand Latin America (describing Bolívar as a Creole aristocrat with Napoleonic vanity), or one believes that Bolívar was an authoritarian politician, defender of lifelong presidencies and hereditary senates, before whom Marx would be almost a liberal democrat. Both variants presume a serious questioning of Bolivarian Marxism.

However, the doctrine of socialism of the twenty-first century can manipulate this and other contradictions, such as the contradiction of claiming 'socialism or barbarism', as expressed by Rosa Luxemburg, which Cornelius Castoriadis and Claude Lefort adopted in postwar Paris. Chávez and his organic intellectuals take on this slogan in a rudimentary way, attributing to it an apocalyptic significance, like that of the *patria o muerte*, 'fatherland or death' of Fidel Castro. However, in Luxemburg just as much as in Lefort and Castoriadis, the 'content of socialism' is contrary to the control of any civil society bureaucracy and for the moment meant, in fact, the opposite of the 'actually existing socialism' of the USSR, Eastern Europe and Cuba, which Lefort and Castoriadis would not have hesitated to consider authoritarian state capitalism.

Official Cuban ideology, which is laid out in the documents of the last Congress of the Communist Party of Cuba in 1997 and in the last meeting of the Central Committee, lacks points of contact with neo-Marxism and subsists in perfect opposition to social democracy, which continues to be understood as yet another variant of liberalism. Faithful to the Soviet inheritance, its theoretical impermeability is such that it can only give in to the rhetoric of Martí's nationalism, a doctrine that, like Chávez's Bolivarianism, would be classified as a collection of bourgeois myths in any kind of critical Marxism. By belonging to the disappeared world of the Soviet order, this ideology is out of place.

The dilemma of many intellectuals on the island who still critically hold up 'socialist' identity (Desiderio Navarro, Víctor Fowler, Julio César Guanche, Arturo Arango, Rafael Hernández, Celia Hart, etc.), wishing to impress upon it an anti-Stalinist or post-Soviet content, is rooted in the fact that, institutionally, Cuban socialism has not stopped being totalitarian. Those intellectuals aspire, therefore, to an 'organicity' that is – if not impossible – only reachable after a regime change to a democratic, leftist government.

To define oneself as a socialist in today's Havana is an attempt to inscribe oneself in a neo-Marxist platform. Ironically, however, this results in a contradictory gesture, because the adjective 'socialist' is assumed by Power as a demonstration of unconditional loyalty. Some of those intellectuals very likely want an opening of the regime or a genuine abandonment of all traces of Stalinism, and may use the 'socialist' label to negotiate narrow margins of agency. But it is evident that the majority thinks that with the 'autocriticism' of the *quinquenio gris*, 'grey five-year period' (1971–6) and the vindication of its victims by the state, the abandonment of Stalinism has already occurred, notwithstanding the single party and planned economy.

The disturbing consensus of the intellectual elites on the island, displayed in the seventh Congress of the National Association of Cuban Writers and Artists (UNEAC) in 2008, bets on a culture directed by the state. What does it mean to be socialist in an intellectual field in which all the writers and artists say they are socialists? Does it only mean this: to share official strategies of resistance to the market? A resistance, certainly, that often means regulation or control of mercantilist mechanisms and not really an opposition to them? When a Cuban intellectual claims to be socialist, it means that he or she accepts a culture that is directed by a political 'vanguard' which in practice is merely a statist bureaucracy which grants the authority to head this 'fight' against the market, without the slightest autonomy of the intellectuals themselves.

The 'socialism with swing' that the poet and essayist Víctor Fowler defended in that Congress is nothing more than an ideology capable of utilizing the skills of the market in its favour and selling it well inside and outside the island. The enterprise that should promote the 'swing' is therefore the state. This is the same enterprise which decides which books are published, which music is listened to, and which art is shown in galleries and museums, in accordance with criteria of aesthetic 'quality'.

The leaders of this business, for example, think that many prizewinning and successful authors in exile, like Zoé Valdés, Eliseo Alberto, Daína Chaviano, Antonio Orlando Rodríguez, José Manuel Prieto or Antonio José Ponte, sell well outside of Cuba because they are 'politicized' and therefore should not be published on the island. The political 'vanguard' of culture fulfills managerial functions that make the state a mediating resort between ideology and the market. The concerted attack against writers who sell best outside the island favours 'revolutionary writers' – equally or more 'politicized' than the exiles – and thereby monopolizes the Latin American editorial market. The same mediating management could be observed in the interested promotion of some kinds of music (*nueva trova, canción latinoamericana, música campesina*) to detract from the market *timba* or *reggaetón*, which are seen as 'vulgar' products, or in the service of media agencies which favour artists coddled by power. The offensive against 'bad taste' in television and popular culture, which we saw in the UNEAC Congress, reveals the persistence of an ideological 'vanguard' which adopts a pedagogical and moralizing role toward the masses.

Let us accept that there exist diverse ways to be socialist in Cuba at the beginning of the twenty-first century. Let us admit that the socialism of the Political Bureau is not identical to that of the few readers of Žižek or Badiou that there are on the island. Let us concede that the official socialism of newspapers and journals like *Granma, Juventud Rebelde* and *La Jiribilla* is one thing and the critical socialism of journals such as *Temas, Criterios* and *La Gaceta de Cuba* is another. Even so, judging by most of their critical interventions, there is a point at which the one coincides with the other: in Cuba, culture is a sphere of the state, subordinate to official ideology. That premise itself, with all its exclusionary logic and the authoritarian bureaucracy, should be the primary focus of debate. However, political hegemony and cultural autonomy, two conceptual pillars of neo-Marxist theory, are not topics of discussion on the island.

Neo-Marxism is a theoretical attitude that, upon being adopted in Havana without a clear gesture of opposition, ends up being distorted. The neo-Marxists, even those who endorse the regime of the island uncritically, like Fredric Jameson or Gianni Vattimo (Jameson and Retamar 2003: 15; see also Vattimo, n.d.), would never accept a single-party system or capitalism of the state in Rome, Paris, London or Washington. In the end, they also know that nothing, neither the commercial embargo nor climate change, nor the 'war against terror', justifies the absence of public liberties in a modern community, but they prefer to make an exception with Cuba because the island is part of the anti-globalization label. The dramatic thing is that this anti-globalization label is endorsed from Havana, a city where all possible socialisms are discarded by the only socialism in power.

Translation by Brooke Hammond-Pérez, Carlos Cañuelas and Shalini Puri

References

Castoriadis, C. (1992) 'The content of socialism', in *Political and Social Writings 1961–1979: Recommencing the Revolution: From Socialism to the Autonomous Society*, Minneapolis: University of Minnesota Press.

Coetzee, J. M. (2008) *Diario de un mal año*, Barcelona: Mondadori.

Jameson, F. and Retamar, R. F. (2003) *Todo Calibán*, San Juan, Puerto Rico: Ediciones Callejón.

Sloterdijk, P. (2005) *En el mundo interior del capital*, Madrid: Siruela.

Vattimo, G. (n.d.) 'Me he convertido al chavismo' (Entrevista) Fuente, online at www.voltairenet.org/article126552.html.

POST-GRENADA, POST-CUBA, POSTCOLONIAL

Rethinking Revolutionary Discourse in Dionne Brand's
In Another Place, Not Here

Raphael Dalleo

Florida Atlantic University, USA

This essay argues for understanding Caribbean postcoloniality as a particular relationship to the Caribbean revolutionary tradition embodied by the Cuban and Grenada revolutions. Looking at how Dionne Brand's In Another Place, Not Here invokes both of those revolutionary moments sheds light on what makes contemporary Caribbean literature postcolonial. In Another Place, Not Here locates itself as a postcolonial text through its relationship to the anticolonial project, both paying homage to and critiquing the limitations of that model. Brand's novel most obviously engages with the legacy of Caribbean revolution through the close resemblances of its unnamed setting to Grenada in the early 1980s; but the novel also directly deploys and rewrites some of the forms of discourse most closely associated with the Cuban Revolution. In particular, the stories of Elizete and Verlia employ two of the genres that came out of Cuba during the 1960s: the testimonio and the story of the intellectual stepping away from privilege to join the revolution. By positioning itself in the aftermath of these milestones in the Caribbean revolutionary tradition, In Another Place, Not Here suggests how we might understand postcolonialism as a simultaneous desire to live up to and critique the political projects of the decolonization era.

1 The 'post' in postcolonial has long left critics asking what exactly postcolonialism is after. Many have pointed to how the term seems to imply the end of imperialism and erases what they often prefer to call neocolonialism; Benita Parry, Anne McClintock and Ella Shohat made some of the earliest and most influential contributions to forcing postcolonialism to address these questions. Shohat's redefinition is most relevant to my own project: 'the *beyond* of postcolonial theory ... seems most meaningful when placed in relation to Third World nationalist discourse. The term *postcolonial* would be more precise, therefore, if articulated as *post-First/Third Worlds theory* or *post-anticolonial critique*, as a movement beyond a relatively binaristic, fixed, and stable mapping of power relations between colonizer/ colonized and centre/ periphery'' (2000: 134). Despite its many shortcomings, *postcolonial* continues to be useful as long as it embodies these many debates and meanings.

What is meant by *postcolonial*? The term suggests a periodization, though when we try to use it in a Caribbean context it seems hard to imagine that it means an era after foreign domination has ended.[1] Politically engaged thought in particular has resisted using the term to describe a region where foreign influence remains so obvious. I suggest a way of periodizing Caribbean literature that does not discard the idea of the postcolonial, but defines it in relation to the history of Caribbean revolutionary movements, in order to keep alive the important lessons that tradition can offer radical politics in the region today. Caribbean postcoloniality can be understood as a 'post-Grenada' experience, as the aftermath of the revolutionary decolonizing project initiated by the Cuban Revolution in 1959 and foreclosed by the US invasion of Grenada in 1983.[2] The work of Dionne Brand sheds particular light on what makes contemporary Caribbean literature postcolonial. Her poetry, her essays and her novel *In Another Place, Not Here* locate themselves as politically engaged postcolonial texts through their relationship to the anticolonial project, paying homage to and critiquing the limitations of that model.

Brand's work points to how theorizing postcoloniality as distinct from the anticolonial moment requires examining the present as a new regime of international domination in which the rethinking of radical politics has required writers to redefine their relationship to the public sphere. In this context, previous forms of opposition and resistance represented by the decolonization struggles of the mid-century provide inspiration but are no longer adequate as models for contemporary struggles in our post-Grenada context. Brand's relationship with Cuba and Grenada aligns her with a broader regional attempt to come to terms with that period's legacies. Writers of decolonization like C. L. R. James, Aimé Césaire and Alejo Carpentier looked to the Haitian Revolution to try to imagine how its successes and failures could speak to their historical moment. Brand is part of a new generation of writers from the 1990s and beyond, such as Julia Alvarez in *In the Name of Salomé*, Elizabeth Nunez in *Beyond the Limbo Silence*, Margaret Cézair-Thompson in *The True History of Paradise*, or Ana Menéndez in *Loving Che*, looking back to the era of decolonization to mourn the loss of the forms of hope that moment presented.[3] The postcolonial is not defined solely negatively, however: the loss of certainty in the narratives of anticolonialism has allowed a productive rethinking of concepts such as the gendering of the revolutionary subject and the relationship of the intellectual to the folk. This essay unpacks the affiliations to the past Brand offers, while considering how the novel imagines the new inspirations the post-Grenada context demands.

Dionne Brand's writing returns over and over to the events that the author participated in during the time she spent in Grenada in 1983. Brand first represents these experiences in the 1984 poetry collection *Chronicles of the*

2 All periodizations are necessarily stories about the past in which certain historical moments are chosen for their symbolic significance. A version of this story solely focused on Cuban faith in revolutionary decolonization might choose the Padilla affair in 1971 or the Mariel boatlift in 1980 as an end point; Latin Americanist versions might choose the 1973 coup in Chile or the electoral defeat of the Sandinistas in 1990 as closing points for this anticolonial period in the Americas. Looking at the relationship of *In Another Place, Not Here* to Cuba serves as a reminder of how the decolonization period was not only transnational but overflowed linguistic boundaries, thus creating periodizations in which Cuba and Grenada become intimately connected.

3 Dalleo and Machado Sáez (2007) focus on how writers such as Alvarez and Menéndez construct a complicated mourning relationship to the Cuban Revolution, as a moment of possibility they wish to affiliate with and recuperate but also feel they no longer can inhabit.

Hostile Sun. These poems describe the horrors of the execution of Maurice Bishop and his comrades, as well as of the US invasion. Her lines are wrought with hopelessness: 'the dream is dead / in these antilles' (Brand 1984: 40), 'the illiterate and oppressed / ... have no words for death, / therefore no real need for life' (49). *Chronicles of the Hostile Sun* apparently closes off the optimistic horizon opened up by revolutionary anticolonialism, as it ends with the poet severed from connection to the people and devoid of any role in their struggles: 'there was no noise / no voice / no radio / none of my companions / things would happen now, without me' (75).

These poems, written in 1983 and 1984, emphasize temporal immediacy. Brand's later work allows a perspective not seen in *Chronicles of the Hostile Sun*, reflecting on what Grenada means for those living in its aftermath. The essay 'Nothing of Egypt' opens with the words 'After Grenada', as the author wanders Ottawa remembering the US invasion (Brand 1994: 131). Living with the wounds opened by that experience is an organizing theme of a number of Brand's essays. These essays are postcolonial, not in the sense that they suggest foreign hegemony has ended in the Caribbean, but because of their attempts to come to terms with a context that has changed. In 'Bathurst', Brand marks the younger version of herself who believed 'I could do anything' as an identity located 'then' (72), and acknowledges that by contrast 'the full press of Black liberation organizing has ground down to a laborious crawl' (77). The essay 'Brownman, Tiger ...' describes a new generation born when 'Fanon was dead, Rodney had already been killed' (102). Despite these losses, though, Brand remains 'hopeful' that 'something's happening' (77). She remembers the pride and sense of purpose the movement provided, as well as the sexism and patriarchal structures it replicated. Whether in the image of the activist's funeral, complete with eulogies (134), or the idea of Grenada as something to be 'mourned' (140), the period of decolonization becomes something to reflect on rather than something to inhabit.

Brand's essay 'Cuba' recalls her decision to go to Grenada, but first opens by remembering her uncle taking a fishing boat to Cuba 'in 1959 or 1960 ... to see what was going on' (Brand 1994: 85). When she runs into that uncle in Grenada in 1983, she realizes that his earlier trip had created her need to get involved: 'Uncle had infected me, jumping into that fishing boat and heading for Cuba, and nothing had felt right until getting there' (96). By 'there' she means Grenada, but also amid the movement to create a Caribbean revolution; for Brand, being in Grenada in 1983 means locating herself within a grand revolutionary tradition. The essay ends with the invasion of Grenada and the writer confronted with the changing historical narrative: 'The headlines ['Communism Dead', 'Death of Communism'] now trumpet the victories of the rich, the weakness of the poor, but I remember Cuba' (99). The construction of this last paragraph contrasts the 'now' of

4 The island where much of *In Another Place, Not Here* is set is never named as Grenada, which Mark McCutcheon (2002) points out allows the experiences described in the novel to take on a representativeness: 'the island assumes an anonymity through which it can stand for the necessity of anti-colonial revolution and that revolution's conflict with those military apparati that so violently strive to repress it (in the name of "American democracy", of course)' (134).
5 Davis's autobiography scrupulously avoids discussions of her closest relationships, especially the romantic or sexual. Davis omits names of friends who helped her while she was a fugitive because of possible legal difficulties they might face. But the avoidance of the personal is also part of a disavowal in the autobiography of the 'illogical' (Davis 1974: 40) and Davis's 'desires' (215); for example, while in prison Davis is critical of how other prisoners pursue sexual relationships with one another, judging 'homosexual fantasy

the New Jewel Movement's failures with a remembered Cuba, able to continue to provide hope. Presenting Cuba as something remembered relegates the still-ongoing Castro government into the past. Cuba is more important in this essay as a symbol of past possibility inspiring future action than as an actually existing present.

Along with Grenada, then, Cuba becomes a central site in Brand's imaginary, as both islands function in the revolutionary imaginary of the region. *In Another Place, Not Here* invokes both islands, Grenada through the events the novel details, but also Cuba through the novel's tropes and generic elements.[4] It tells two stories, of Verlia and of Elizete, and in the process participates in two genres closely associated with the Cuban Revolution: (1) the story of the intellectual stepping away from privilege to join the revolution and (2) the *testimonio*. The idea of the intellectual aligning with the people through downward mobility has a long history in Caribbean narrative, going back to Claude McKay's *Banana Bottom*, C. L. R. James's *Minty Alley*, and Jacques Roumain's *Masters of the Dew*. In association with the Cuban Revolution this trajectory is specifically captured in stories of intellectuals showing commitment to revolution by participating in cane-cutting brigades. Closest to Verlia's story are the narratives of North American or Latin American intellectuals travelling to Cuba to participate in its revolution: Angela Davis's account of her work in the cane fields in the Cuban section of her autobiography is perhaps the most famous. In this context, Verlia sweating and wielding a machete alongside Elizete is the diasporic intellectual who must reroot herself in the island through working the soil and proving her solidarity with the peasantry.

Focusing on the writer's need to enact this rerooting allows these narratives to avoid the idea of the intellectual as bearer of knowledge coming to save the downtrodden natives. Although Elizete credits Verlia with helping 'wake me up' to her male lover's abusive oppressiveness (Brand 1996: 6), the novel shows Verlia to be driven by her own desires and learning process. In particular, the novel depicts in Verlia's journeys a desire for inhabiting the public sphere and a flight from the private. In exploring this desire, Brand thematizes the anticolonial ideas of public and private as they pertain to a black woman, invoking the same problematic as *Angela Davis: An Autobiography*, which performs an exaggerated presentation of its subject as a purely rational, genderless intellect.[5]

In Brand's novel, Verlia exhibits ambivalence towards the private: she leaves Toronto and her lover because 'she needed a mission outside of herself', feeling that there is 'nothing more hopeless than two people down to themselves for company' (Brand 1996: 97) and that 'I couldn't just live in a personal thing' (102). The issue for Verlia is not just being acknowledged by a public sphere where she is triply excluded as a queer black woman. Even more, Verlia seeks a kind of solidarity that can only be expressed through the life' as another 'attractive channel for escape' (55) like movies, the commissary, church, or 'bad literature whose sole function was to create emotional paths of escape' (51).

'immolating of oneself' (207), as in the passage from Fanon she remembers: 'The colonialist bourgeoisie has hammered into the native's mind the idea of a society of individuals where each person shut himself up in his own subjectivity' (159). *In Another Place, Not Here* attempts to enact this breaking down of individual subjectivities through its style: Ellen Quigley shows that the use of pronouns and shifting perspectives helps the novel 'deconstruct identity politics and produce new heterogeneous subjectivity' (2005: 49). Yet within Verlia's narrative, this deconstruction of individuality is also a suppression of her own desires, a denial of herself as a biological being that has the practical effect of sending her back to the closet. The part of her self she seeks to eliminate is the realm of feelings: in decorating her room, for example, 'she wants it bare ... No photographs, no sentiment, no memory' (Brand 1996: 156).

The split of intellect and feeling is nowhere clearer than when Abena worries that Verlia's nervous breakdowns come from working underground; Verlia replies, 'It's just my body. My head's straight' (191). Verlia's problem is always her body. It forces her to be aware of the personal, keeping her from being 'straight'. It prevents the leap into a future not weighed down by the past that Verlia longs for and finally makes: the novel's final scene describes Elizete watching Verlia 'running, turning, leap off a cliff' (246) until 'her body has fallen away' (247). But this leap leaves behind Elizete and the others Verlia set out to help. The body ultimately can't be abandoned. Verlia assembles newspaper clippings to create a public past to take the place of her personal background: 'bits of newspapers are her history, words her family' (164). Yet working amid the revolution, she continues to think about Abena and her family: in her diary, she records thinking of them and how 'I feel so small ... it weakens me to think of them' (213). Remembering Abena produces the same effect: 'I called Abena and became sad ... She sounded sad. My imagination or my period' (208). Emotion, here dismissed as feminine and biological, presents a threat to the rational public persona Verlia seeks to create.

Yet in keeping a diary, this most personal form of writing, Verlia shows the potential function of the private. The novel deconstructs the opposition of intellect as public and emotion as private by framing solidarity through the passage from Che Guevara that Verlia returns to: 'She wants to live in Che's line ... "At the risk of seeming ridiculous, let me say that the true revolutionary is guided by great feelings of love"' (Brand 1996: 165). The form of love Verlia strives for is an abstracted, rationalized love of the people in general; Guevara's next sentences ask that 'revolutionaries idealize this love of the people' but not 'descend, with small doses of daily affection, to the level where ordinary people put their love into practice' (Guevara 2003: 226). *In Another Place, Not Here* shows the boundaries between these two forms of love breaking down. Verlia's love of Elizete is for her as a person as well as for the oppressed peasantry she represents: the sexualized gaze which Verlia casts on her at work shows the intellectual 'in love with the arc of a woman's arm, long and one with a cutlass, slicing a cane stalk' (Brand 1996: 203). This embodied love allows Verlia to begin to 'come close to the people' and establish the grounds for her solidarity with them (203).

Verlia's mode of enacting that rerooting, through a sexual relationship with a peasant, rehearses a common trope of anticolonial writing that Brand criticizes in the essay 'This Body for Itself'. She argues that the anticolonial novel in which the intellectual fascination with the peasantry becomes played out through a sexual relationship uses the black woman's body as object for the intellectual male's redemption. Brand writes of Roumain's *Masters of the Dew*: 'Here it is the woman as country, virginal, unspoiled land, as territory for anti-colonial struggle ... their approach to the Black female body is as redeemer of the violated' (Brand 1994: 35). Elizete represents for Verlia the terrain of her rerooting just as Annaïse becomes the land for Manuel in *Masters of the Dew*. Yet *In Another Place, Not Here* offers something absent from *Minty Alley* or *Masters of the Dew*: the perspective of Maisie and Annaïse. The narrators of those novels take the point of view of their intellectual protagonists, while *In Another Place, Not Here* reverses that gaze in opening with Elizete's voice. Elizete is allowed to express resistance to any political project that depends on her objectification, resisting Verlia's desire to know and understand her: 'I tell she I not no school book with she, I not no report card, I not no exam' (77).

By the time of the Cuban Revolution, the anticolonial mode of establishing solidarity had begun to be challenged for reproducing the privileged position of the intellectual as heroic actor in the revolutionary story. The *testimonio* meant to create a new relationship between intellectual and folk through positing a new narrative subject. The genre was inaugurated with the publication of Miguel Barnet's *Biografía de un cimarrón* in Cuba in 1966; in 1973 the Casa de las Américas canonized the genre by creating a separate category for *testimonio* among their annual prizes. Instead of focusing on the intellectual longing to be one with the people seen in anticolonial writing like *Banana Bottom* or *Minty Alley*, the *testimonio* suggests that the professional writer's role in postcolonial society should be to give over the space of the page to the illiterate and excluded, to give up the aura of creator and act purely as translator for the oral tales of the folk.[6] Barnet describes *testimonio* as a story of a 'representative protagonist'; these protagonists, 'without having chosen to be, are also witnesses, but real witnesses in a sociological rather than a strictly literary sense' (1981: 21). Through telling the true stories of these witnesses, the professional writer enables 'the suppression of the writer's *I* or the sociologist's ego' in order to 'become a part of the psychology of the people' (22). *Testimonio* thus speaks directly in the voice of an uneducated, marginalized person who represents the ordinary rather

6 In the anglophone Caribbean of the 1960s and 1970s the same testimonial impulse can be seen in the repositioning of performance through the work of Derek Walcott and Trevor Rhone, Mervyn Morris's championing of Louise Bennett, a film like *The Harder They Come*, and most especially the Sistren Theatre Collective.

than unique experience and requires the professional writer only because he or she does not have the ability to write the story for him- or herself.

Although not exactly the non-fiction *testimonio* built around interviewing real people practised by Barnet, *In Another Place, Not Here* begins in Elizete's voice, invoking the testimonial strategy by allowing readers to experience the Grenadian Revolution through the eyes not of an intellectual but an uneducated peasant. This point of view may seemingly lack the big picture of history, but its allusiveness uses other ways to get at underlying truths. For example, while Elizete describes her ancestor's arrival in the Caribbean, she is unable to name the experience as what traditional history might call the Middle Passage (Brand 1996: 18–21), but the oral history she has inherited allows her to recount this past in the same imagistic and metaphorical way that the narrator of *Biografía de un cimarrón*, Esteban Montejo, narrates the history of slavery (Barnet 1994: 18). Both Elizete and Montejo are presented as inhabiting an organic, epic world that can seem almost prelinguistic – Montejo's narrative makes no distinction between history, religion, folktale and his everyday life, while Elizete admits that while she knows and understands how to use many of the plants on the island, 'I don't know their names' (Brand 1996: 17). These voices are thus simultaneously naïve but filled with insight, embodying an alternative archive that the professional writer and literary reader must learn from.

At the same time that *In Another Place, Not Here* connects to these two genres of Caribbean writing aligned with the era of decolonization and the Cuban Revolution, the novel deploys these genres in ways which challenge their basic assumptions. The *testimonio* simultaneously expresses a post-colonial impulse in seeking to erase the presence of the professional writer, contributing to the illusion of the folk subject speaking without mediation, even while prefaces and author's notes remind the reader of the heroic anticolonial work the professional writer has done in finding and recording this story. The ideal is, as Jean Franco puts it, that in *testimonio* 'the intellectual virtually disappears from the text in order to let "the subaltern speak"' (1999: 54); the reality is that the intellectual whose position in the public sphere has been challenged can reassert authority through the *testimonio*. Barnet is again typical, beginning *Biografía* with an introduction (not included in the English translation) describing his own process of finding Esteban Montejo and bringing his story to the page. Barnet's reflections on methodology continue this paradoxical attempt to both aver the need to undermine the privilege of the writer as well as create a new heroic role for the writer, calling for the suppression of the writer's ego while advocating that the writer can through *testimonio* 'contribute to an under-standing of reality' unlike what fiction accomplishes (Barnet 1981: 23). Thus within the *testimonio*, the presence of the professional writer disappears – nowhere does Montejo mention Barnet in his narrative – even while paratextual elements conjure back into existence that presence and reinforce its authority.

Brand's novel does not allow the presence of the intellectual to remain unexamined; Elizete and Verlia exist in relation to one another, neither one privileged. *In Another Place, Not Here* thus becomes about the relationship of intellectual and folk as a narrative of desire, but one where the desire of the folk is actually explored. From the first chapter, the novel makes Elizete a desiring subject. Just as Verlia's desires for Elizete become embedded in her abstracted need for union with the folk, we see Elizete's desires for Verlia as reflective of her own larger dreams: 'she looked like the young in me, the not beaten down and bruised' (15). Elizete sees her own potential in Verlia, and their relationship becomes a way of realizing herself. Putting the two narratives together makes them exist in relation with one another, calling into question the romantic vision of the folk representing the absolute alterity that drives revolutionary opposition, as well as the presentation of the intellectual as heroic but isolated vanguardist leaping ahead of the people. The existence of these two characters on a continuum is nowhere more apparent than in Elizete's journey to Toronto, where she shows the folk subject becoming as mobile and cosmopolitan as the intellectual. In her travel, Elizete takes the position of enlightenment seeker searching to 'know' the city where she arrives even if 'somehow this place resisted knowing' (69).

This dialectic, between the subject wanting to know and the object that resists being known, typifies European colonial writing as much as anticolonial narratives of the intellectual encounter with the folk. Arriving in Canada, Elizete is described in terms that reverse that encounter: 'today she was Columbus' (47). But the encounter model becomes even blurrier: Elizete and Verlia exchange these positions, each seeking to know the other and each resisting being known. Making this story one of same-sex desire, and giving each of the women their own portion of the narrative, places the exploration of their desires on a more equal footing. Verlia is frustrated by her inability to recognize her surroundings or feel at home: 'things grow so fast I hardly recognize some roads and paths any more' (219). As in *Minty Alley*, Verlia forges a relationship with Elizete in order to be connected to the place, but can never know Elizete's experience or perspective as completely as she desires. The novel also makes Verlia the object of Elizete's fascination to know: 'I used to wonder who she went home to ... wondered if she was the same in town, what she kitchen smell like ... Soon I was only wondering about she' (9–10). Elizete's journey to Toronto and desire to cognitively map this city to connect with her lost lover directly replicates Verlia's equating of Caribbean space with the folk subject.

Both characters express desire to overcome the boundaries separating them. But neither character is able to fully understand the other, let alone become other herself. Ultimately, 'there was a distance between them that was inescapable and what they did not talk about. At times [Elizete] saw someone she did not know in Verlia. ... How could she know Verlia' (54). What finally stands between them is the same thing Verlia tries to sublimate in her section of the narrative: the body which each occupies and can never be occupied by the other, even if sexual union comes closest to realizing that desire. For Elizete, too, the body is an unwelcome reminder of her history: 'Heavy as hell. Her body. She doesn't want a sense of it while she's living on the street. She doesn't think of the scars on her legs, she doesn't hide them, she doesn't think of Verlia touching them' (54). Just as the biological realities of personal needs and desires keep Verlia from successfully leaping into an unmoored future, not shaped by a past of suffering, the body weighs down Elizete and marks the possibilities available for her. The novel suggests all of these aspects of the body as that which the anticolonial narrative of revolutionary redemption most desires to overcome, but cannot totally leap out of.

In Another Place, Not Here thus reveals itself to be a postcolonial text through its desire to both inhabit and critique the narrative of revolutionary decolonization represented by figures like Angela Davis and Esteban Montejo. While the stories of Verlia and Elizete invoke these anticolonial predecessors, there is a third character in the novel: Abena. The lover who initiated Verlia into the movement, Abena represents another possibility for the intellectual who did not choose Verlia's self-immolating path. Abena doesn't join Verlia because 'she'd been paralysed' (238), and while Verlia's story is marked by movement and taking action, the novel's penultimate chapter explores Abena falling into stasis. Verlia judges Abena harshly, not so different from the 'sellouts' who argue for 'going slow' (177). Abena won't commit to revolutionary action because, Verlia suspects, 'maybe Abena was hiding something, maybe there was some reason that wasn't really about the struggle at all but personal' (186).

Despite Verlia's continued insistence on enforcing the boundaries of the private and public in thinking of Abena this way, the novel has already shown that even Verlia's involvement in the movement fulfills for her both personal as well as political needs. What we ultimately see in Abena is a reoriented intellectual project, not organized around heroic contests for power but the everyday struggle to help ordinary people. Abena is tempted by hopelessness, scoffs to herself 'as if anybody would dream' in the aftermath of what she has seen (229). But she hasn't completely given up. Abena is part of the 'something happening' that Brand describes in the essays from *Bread Out of Stone*, as 'people figure out how to do the day-to-day so that life's not so hard' (Brand 1994: 77): '[Verlia] didn't know how Abena kept it up, just content to break the rules, a passport here for someone running, a car to Buffalo, a health card, a pay cheque under the table. Small things, Abena said, small things are the only things you can do sometimes' (Brand 1996: 193). In ending with Abena in dialogue with Elizete as the two try to come to terms with Verlia the intellectual-as-saviour as well as their own identities as women and political actors, *In Another Place, Not Here* posits the central questions of postcoloniality: of what kind of relationship Abena and Elizete can forge, and of what kind of new political projects that alliance can work towards in the face of apparent defeat. While Verlia's anticolonial dreams animate much of the action of *In Another Place, Not Here*, the novel ends by wondering what her legacy means to those she has left behind.

References

Barnet, M. (1981) 'The documentary novel', *Cuban Studies/Estudios Cubanos* 11(1): 19–32.

Barnet, M. (1994) [1966] *Biography of a Runaway Slave*, trans. N. Hill, East Haven, CT: Curbstone Press.

Brand, D. (1984) *Chronicles of the Hostile Sun*, Toronto: Williams-Wallace Publishers.

Brand, D. (1994) *Bread Out Of Stone*, Toronto: Coach House Press.

Brand, D. (1996) *In Another Place, Not Here*, New York: Grove Press.

Dalleo, R. and Machado Sáez, E. M. (2007) *The Latino/a Canon and the Emergence of Post-Sixties Literature*, New York: Palgrave Macmillan.

Davis, A. (1974) *Angela Davis: An Autobiography*, New York: International Publishers.

Franco, J. (1999) 'Going public: reinhabiting the private', in M. L. Pratt and K. Newman (eds) *Critical Passions: Selected Essays*, Durham, NC: Duke University Press, pp. 48–65.

Guevara, E. (2003) [1965] 'Socialism and man in Cuba', in D. Deutschmann (ed.) *Che Guevara Reader*, New York: Ocean Press, pp. 212–28.

McClintock, A. (1992) 'The angel of progress: pitfalls of the term "post-colonialism"', *Social Text* 31/32: 84–98.

McCutcheon, M. (2002) 'She skin black as water: The movement of liquid imagery in Dionne Brand's *In Another Place, Not Here*', *Post Identity* 3 (2): 133–52.

Parry, B. (1987) 'Problems in current theories of colonial discourse', *Oxford Literary Review* 9(1–2): 27–58.

Quigley, E. (2005) 'Picking the deadlock of legitimacy: Dionne Brand's "noise like the world cracking"', *Canadian Literature* 186: 48–68.

Shohat, E. (2000) [1992] 'Notes on the "Post-Colonial"', in F. Afzal-Khan and K. Seshadri-Crooks (eds) *The Pre-Occupation of Postcolonial Studies*, Durham, NC: Duke University Press, pp. 126–39.

Maps by Annalee Davis

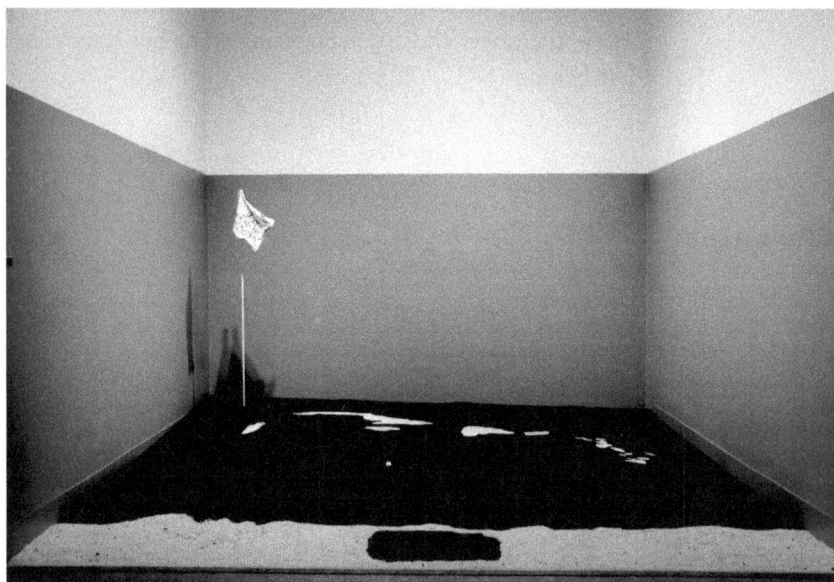

"Just Beyond My Imagination"
Installation: indoor/outdoor carpeting, cast plaster, sand, engraved red carpet, flagpole with embroidered flag, golf ball. Size: 15'w × 12'd × 10' h.
Artist's Private Collection
Photo Credit: Remy Jungerman
2007

"Undocumented migrant "
Still from "On the Map"
a Documentary Video Project by Annalee Davis
2007
Photo Credit: Omar Estrada

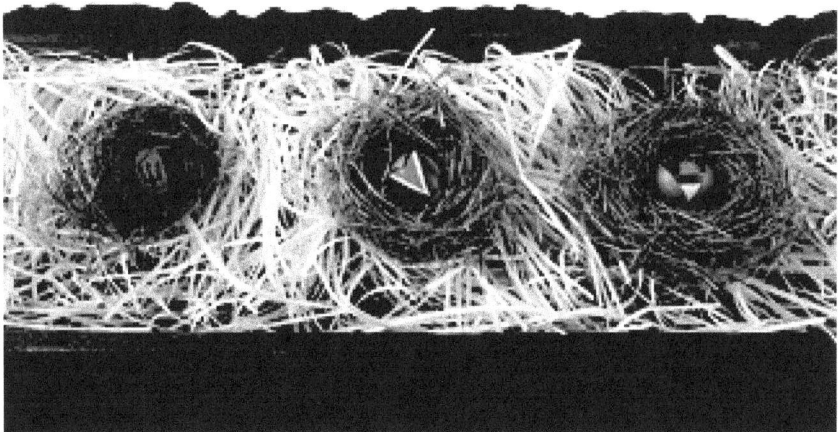

"Hatchlings - A Requiem", (Detail) 2009
Installation: velvet, shredded Revised Treaty of Chaguaramas, fifteen nests, acrylic on fifteen chicken eggs.
13"w × 12'd × 35"h
Artist's Private Collection
Photo Credit: Dan Christaldi

HISTORY, DECOLONIZATION AND THE MAKING OF REVOLUTION

Reflections on Writing the Popular History of the Jamaican Events of 1938

Anthony Bogues
Brown University, USA

The writing of popular history in Jamaica has a tradition which begins inside the anticolonial movement and develops with the Marxist Left in the 1970s. This essay examines how the major texts of this tradition describe the historical 1938 events. It suggests that while the tradition foregrounded popular movements, it did so within frames which negated the political ideas of these groups. In the end the essay argues for a critical subaltern historiography which pays attention to political thought and the frames in which they may be expressed.

> We are the sons of slaves who have been paying rent to landlords for fully many decades. We want better wages, we have been exploited for years ... we want freedom in this the hundredth year of our emancipation. (Petition of Poor Man's Improvement Land Settlement and Labour Association, April 1938)

The rebellions of 1937–8 in Jamaica and the Caribbean have been widely interpreted as the dawn of political modernity for the region. As such, debates over their meaning are relevant to the entire region. Moreover, they

1 The 1938 events should really be viewed as a regional mass uprising which begins with the 1935 oilfield workers of the Trinidad hunger march led by Uriah Butler. Between 1935 and 1938 there were numerous strikes and mass protests in the anglophone Caribbean, which shook the British colonial system. The colonial office responded by establishing the Moyne Commission to investigate the conditions that led to mass protest and strikes. For an overview of the strikes and mass protest, see Bolland (2001).

2 For further discussion of how the narratives of creole nationalism suppress the discussions of other forms of nationalisms in Jamaica during the early twentieth century and what this means for interpretation of 1938, see Bogues (2002).

starkly illustrate the complexity of the relationship between conventional revisionist and popular history.[1]

It is conventionally argued and consensually agreed by historians of all political stripes that modern political parties, trade unions and the shape of the modern Jamaican political system emerged as direct consequences of the 1938 events. For the creole nationalist, 1938 was the birth of the anticolonial movement, and for the political Left it marked the most massive resistance to colonial domination and a singular event which demonstrated working-class activity and capacity for mass action that could potentially transform a society.[2]

The publication in 1939 of Arthur Lewis's *Labour in the West Indies: The Birth of a Workers' Movement* consolidated the naming of the 1938 events as a workers' revolt. Published in England by the Fabian Society a few months after the upsurge, the book opened a path of historical analysis which continues to dominate the historical meanings of the mass rebellions of the period. A. Creech Jones (who in 1946 became the colonial secretary for the British colonies) claimed in his preface to the book, 'These people have come into the European tradition of culture and labour. The organizations are still confused and muddling. They make mistakes and are sometimes poorly led. But there is a surge forward of a working class' (Lewis 1977: 10). There is in Jones's argument the colonial assumption of tutelage, as the colonial child struggles through colonial mimicry towards adulthood. But what is more intriguing is how the assumptions about the maturity or lack thereof of the Jamaican working class in the early twentieth century would come to undergird nationalist renderings of the 1938 Jamaican events.

Lewis's book is primarily a compendium of economic and social facts focusing on the degrading conditions of agricultural workers' wages, health and housing. The book presents a brief history of early trade union organizations in all of the islands and concludes with a section entitled 'What can be done?' which prescribes a set of policy measures for the colonial office to implement. It closes with the following sentences:

> The Labour Movement is on the march. It has already behind it a history of great achievement in a short space of time. It will make of the West Indies of the future a country where the common man may lead a cultured life in freedom and prosperity. (52)

Unlike the British colonial office, which labelled the rebellion as 'disturbances', Lewis located the rebellion as the climax of workers' and nascent trade union activity in the region, and fixed the appellation of 'workers' rebellion' on the regional events (Lamming and Paquet 2001). Thenceforth, the 1938 events were conceptualized primarily as the progressive march of labour. From this frame both nationalists and radicals would return to the 1938 events as *the* touchstone for different currents of Jamaican politics. To put the issue another way, oftentimes the question would be posed in Jamaican political discourse: what kind of politics was required to inherit the mantle of 1938?

The Emergence of a Tradition

Academic scholarship about Jamaican historical writing has largely neglected political pamphlets and explicitly activist historiography emerging out of radical political practices. However, from the 1950s through the 1970s in Jamaica, there existed a vibrant tradition of such popular historical writing. To my mind, the most important figure in the emergence of this tradition was Richard Hart.

Richard Hart is one of the four H's who were expelled from the People's National Party in 1952.[3] A lawyer by training, Hart adopted Marxist-Leninist political positions in the 1930s and by 1937, along with Hugh Buchanan, A. A. Morris and Osmond Dyce, formed the Marxist Left Group (MLG). In 1938 with the formation of the People's National Party, Hart became part of the PNP Left.[4]

The MLG's political perspective was of a two-staged approach. The first stage was the anticolonial struggle in which the interests of labour was subsumed. In the course of his organizational work, Hart began to notice that at mass political meetings he received rapt attention whenever he referred to episodes of Jamaican history in which slaves, ex-slaves or ordinary people rebelled, especially when he spoke about the leader of the 1831 slave rebellion, Sam Sharpe. Hart recalls that initially the leadership of the PNP (Norman Manley and others) did not see the importance of his invocations of slave rebellions (Hart 1980: i). But Hart began to think about and write specific histories of Jamaican slave revolts, and by the early 1950s had produced a major booklet on Jamaican history, *The Origin and Development of the People of Jamaica*. In the 1972 edition of the booklet he argued that while it dealt primarily with the 'history of the labour force', he believed 'plantation owners and their top managerial staff ... thought of themselves as Englishmen overseas [and] that the black slaves ... despite their involuntary migration from Africa, constituted of necessity the embryo of the Jamaican nation' (Hart 1972: 2).

Originally published in 1952 by the education unit of the Trade Union Congress in Jamaica, Hart's booklet was extensively used in general worker and political education programmes by unions and in some instances by the PNP. Hart's primary aim was to recount a historical narrative in which Jamaican history was not a smooth story of colonial

3 The other persons expelled were Frank Hill, Ken Hill and Arthur Henry. For a description of the political issues involved in the expulsion, see Hart (2004).

4 For a discussion of this group and its activity within the PNP before 1952, see Munroe (1977).

5 The figure of Richard Hart is in dire need of a political biography. Hart has claimed that his major historical works are his two volumes, *Slaves Who Abolished Slavery* (1980). The popular historical writings of Hart are very important in any overall consideration of Caribbean historical writing. Elsa Goveia, perhaps the most important figure in the development of a Caribbean historiography, recounts in 1969 that the first conferences

occupation wherein slave plantations civilized the 'nativized' slave and colonial subject. Instead, he furnished a story of struggle and resistance to slavery and colonial domination within a narrative that folded slave resistance into worker rebellions and trade union organizations. Thus, for Hart, the central feature of the history of the Jamaican people was their heroic resistance against racial slavery, and then with the shift in the mode of capital accumulation and labour exploitation, this heroic resistance folded into the birth of workers' organizations in the late nineteenth and early twentieth centuries. Constructing a historical narrative of struggle and resistance, Hart formulated a political argument about the necessity of social and political struggles to achieve independence as a continuation of a historical legacy. However, what is crucial for our purposes here is that he inaugurates a tradition which has been neglected in accounts of Jamaican historical writing: a tradition in which radical political practice becomes inseparable from the writing of history.[5] A detailed critique of the silences in Hart's text is beyond the scope of this essay, but Hart is exemplary of many other radical historians and political activists in treating 1938 as the demise of colonial domination and the inauguration of Jamaican political modernity.

Marxism and the Historical Narratives of 1938

to discuss increased teaching of West Indian history in high schools occurred in 1956. These conferences led to the writing of the very important text by Roy Augier and Shirley Gordon (1962). Hart's booklet was published four years before these conferences. For an account of the emergence of Caribbean history and its teaching, see Augier (2008) and Higman (1999).

6 See also the popular song by the reggae group the Ethiopians,

In the late 1960s and mid-1970s two texts appeared which still remain exemplars of popular historical writings deployed for explicit political objectives: Ken Post's 1969 article on 1938 which appeared in the radical Jamaican newspaper *Abeng*, and the Workers Liberation League's (WLL) pamphlet first written by Don Robotham, *Our Struggles*. For Ken Post, the 1938 rebellion was an instance in which 'the workers and peasants in Jamaica really did stand up to the colonial system … so it was well worth it … devoting a study to that topic' (Scott 1998; see also Bogues 1998). An English political scientist, Post was initially trained as an Africanist and had come to Jamaica as part of the British Overseas Development programme to teach at the University of the West Indies. He arrived in Jamaica when postcolonial protest was at a fever pitch, as Black Power, Rastafari, urban subalterns, students, unemployed and workers began to overtly challenge the elite domination of the Jamaican neocolonial state (Lewis 1998).[6]

The vibrancy of this political moment was to have a profound effect on Ken Post as he forged links and developed his political practice in Jamaica. During this period he was associated with the radical newspaper *Abeng*, which had emerged out of the Walter Rodney Riots in Jamaica in October 1968.[7] As a writer for the newspaper, his initial focus was on the African

Everything Crash.
One cannot examine
Jamaican history
without any serious
discussion of
Jamaican popular
music, particularly as
a subaltern cultural/
political practice.

7 For a discussion of
the political ideas of
the newspaper, see
Bogues (2010). For
Post's own
understanding and
recounting of his
Jamaican experience,
see the interview
between himself and
David Scott in *Small
Axe* 4: 85–157. Post
also seems to have
dabbled in forming a
small guerrilla
movement.

8 See *Abeng* 1 (17 &
18), 3 and 24 May
1969; see also Post
(1969).

national liberation movements. He wrote two pieces on the 1938 rebellion: one was published in *Abeng* and the other in the academic journal *Social and Economic Studies*.[8]

Abeng attempted to mobilize around issues of unemployment, police brutality, workers' rights and corruption in the Jamaican neocolonial state. With its front-page banner taken from a Marcus Garvey speech, 'We want our people to think for themselves', the newspaper aspired to be a vehicle for mass popular political education. The front page blurb which introduced Post's article proclaims: 'Inside: May 1938. What we need to know.' The blurb was placed beside a picture of a massive crowd on the streets clearly either waiting in anticipation of something to happen or standing around after an event has already occurred. Post writes his article on 1938 under the name 'Historian' and begins by asking the question, 'What happened in Jamaica in May and June 1938?' He offers answers which argue that although the outbreak was part of a regional occurrence, in Jamaica the events were more 'widespread and prolonged ... during that three weeks the whole colonial system was under severest pressure, and it can be argued that not until 5 June did the administration really show signs of being able to handle the situation in terms other than brute force' (*Abeng* 1 (17) 1969).

Post repudiates the colonial myth of the satisfied 'native', refuting colonial descriptions of the Jamaican colonized and the 'good temper of the labouring classes' thus:

> What these good-tempered people were in fact doing was blocking roads, cutting telephone wires, breaking down bridges, burning cane, destroying banana trees and, on several occasions, ambushing armed police with nothing but sticks and stones. Given arms, ideology and different leaders the story might have been quite a different one. (Ibid.)

Yet, although Post illustrates the defiance of those who rebelled, he is still wedded to a certain view about the ultimate goals of the mass action. Thus, for Post, three things were missing from the rebellion: arms, ideology and leadership. Within the framework of Marxist revolutionary theory all these three were necessary for successful revolution. What this meant was that in a Marxist analysis, the events of 1938 were interpreted from the standpoint of the *inability* of the actors to make a revolution and not from the standpoint of the internal dynamics and logics of the events itself.

In perhaps the strongest section of the article, Post attempts to answer another question which he posed, 'Who were the demonstrators?' In a detailed analysis of the various social groups active during this period, he pays special attention to one group which unsettles the overarching conception of the rebellion as a 'workers' rebellion'. Focusing on the activities of a group he calls the 'banana workers', Post notes:

> It was the banana carriers in the hinterland who were the intransigents, bringing the whole industry to a halt by rolling strikes which would start on one plantation and then spread for miles as the workers marched from plantation to plantation bringing out the rest. ... Nevertheless, it is not primarily as wage workers that the banana carriers must be seen but as peasant farmers. (Ibid.)

Here we come upon one of the major conundrums which faced Marxist social analysis in Jamaica and the Caribbean. How can one describe the Jamaican ex-slave who both worked on his/her own land and also worked on the banana or sugar plantations? Post's answer was to begin with the social category of worker and then complicate this by suggesting that this worker was really a peasant farmer. The issue was a fundamental one, since it was about modes of classification and economic productive activity. In the 1970s different categories were used to describe the structure and operation of the Jamaican economy. These ranged from semi-feudal to (perhaps most influentially) the plantation society economic model developed primarily by the New World Group (Girvan and Meeks 2010).

My point here is that the major social categories deployed in the popular education article aimed at the dominated sectors were not rooted in their social reality. It is therefore deeply ironic that this article and particular forms of analysis were performed under the banner 'We want our people to think for themselves'. Post finally concludes the first part of his article with the major point that the 1938 rebellion was a 'mass uprising', not just a worker rebellion. This was an important discursive shift, but there was still unsettled business: what was the character of this 'mass uprising' and, more importantly, what were its meanings and how should we interpret it?

In the second part of the article, Post points to the influence of Garveyism on the rebellion and then notes something extraordinarily important: 'I know of only one instance of explicit Rastafarian participation in the events of May-June 1938, there is no doubt that this aspect of the consciousness of the masses requires very careful study' (*Abeng* 1 (18) 31 May 1969).

Here we begin to get possible clues as to some of the elements which might have been critical to grappling with the interior ideology of the mass uprising. In his 1978 publication about the rebellion, *Arise Ye Starvelings*, Post pays great attention to black consciousness. In a remarkable chapter entitled 'Ethiopia Stretches Forth Her Hands', he characterizes one stream of black consciousness as 'Jamaican Ethiopianism'. Post observes that by 1937 'Jamaican Ethiopianism' had formed itself as an ideology. However, deeply influenced by Althusser's structural Marxism and theory of ideology, Post argues that Ethiopianism was a 'false consciousness because it spoke of biblical myths and events and other remote (often pseudo-) historical material, not of the Jamaican class structure and its relations'. He then ends: 'In that sense there was far too small a rational kernel within its mystical shell' (Post 1978: 193). Instead of studying this 'ideology' and how it developed a local politico-religious outlook which challenged the colonial order, Post reduces the most important Afro-Jamaican politico-religious practices to emerge in late nineteenth-century and early twentieth-century Jamaica to lower-level irrational musings unable to come to grips with the island's class structure.

Thus, though he presents detailed empirical evidence which would allow us to change our understanding of the Jamaican 1938 events from that of 'workers' rebellion' to 'mass uprising', Post is unable to come to grips with the one element of the ideology which propelled the uprising. His is a methodology of 'history from below', but one which still remains wedded to a voiceless subaltern. To further illustrate this we should note that Post in his 1978 book does not take up his own injunction to pay more attention to Rastafari during the 1938 events.

Post ends his article on 1938 by wondering whether the events of 1938 were rebellion or a revolution. In answering, he argues that those who rebelled accepted

> the prevailing social values ... what they are seeking to do, in fact, is to restore those values – or, more accurately, an idealized version of them. ... Revolution-aries, on the other hand, assert against existing values a counter-consciousness with values of its own ... two essential prerequisites were missing from the situation if revolution in fact were to come about – a new consciousness on the part of the sufferers which they could oppose to the existing values and an organization to lead them. (*Abeng* 1 (18) 31 May 1969)

But this asserted gap between rebellion and revolution does not take into account the ways in which counter-hegemonic blocs are formed. It is also unaware of how political language functions, how similar words come to mean different things to different social groups. Moreover, Post's words reveal again that preoccupation with leadership, which holds that the failure to cross the rubicon from rebellion to revolution resides in leadership. This kind of historical analysis is unable to understand events for what they are and might be. In part this is due to the fact that the writer's desire for a particular kind of revolution (a worthy and important desire) sometimes clouds his gaze. If revolution can *only* be explained in Marxist categories, then explanation for failure must be found in these terms. I would suggest that this kind of historical interpretation misses the richness and complex-ities of an event.

Rebellion or Revolution?

If Ken Post was of the opinion that the 1938 events were both a rebellion and a mass uprising, then the other major popular publication on the event – published six years later – also wrestled with the character of the 1938 events. *Our Struggles*, written by Don Robotham and published by the Workers' Liberation League, argued:

> Workers lacking political experience, weak in organization, without any clear revolutionary ideology, with no set programme and no tactics and no developed programme, were guided by their instincts. But theirs were revolutionary instincts born from years of bitter suffering and they pointed the workers to their chief oppressors – the imperialists and the local barons. (Robotham 1975: 86)

9 Alexander Bustamante was the founder of both the Jamaica Labour Party and the Bustamante Industrial Trade Union. Beginning as a reformist labour leader, he was politically conservative and by the time he became Jamaica's first prime minister he proclaimed with great delight and ease, 'We are with the West.' For a political biography of Bustamante, see Eaton (1975).

10 I am not talking about C. L. R. James's *Black Jacobins* in this essay, in part because it was an anticolonial

The differences between Post's assessment of the events and the WLL's were not significant. Both operated from within currents of Marxism. However, these Marxist paradigms were ones in which the specific historical contours of Caribbean and Jamaican societies were not given full play. In Post's language, the event was a rebellion because the rebels lacked a 'counter-consciousness with values of its own'. And here we should pause to remind ourselves whether or not Ethiopianism was not a counter-consciousness with a different set of values than those of the colonial order. For the WLL, the workers had no clear revolutionary ideology. Both writers agreed that there was a problem of leadership and organization. For the WLL, an index of the lack of revolutionary ideology and leadership was that the workers accepted the leadership of Alexander Bustamante.[9] In Robotham's view the primary reason for the lack of revolutionary leadership was that 'the bulk of our proletariat was an agrarian one, living under relations of production which were semi-proletarian and semi-tenant in character, above all crushed by the power of land monopoly' (1975: 89). One consequence of lack of leadership combined with agrarian relations was in Robotham's eyes that the workers failed to make 'a capitalist democratic revolution – one which would open the way to the rapid development of capitalism and thus open the way to socialism' (ibid.). This kind of historical reasoning in which an event is judged by a teleological frame meant that Robotham presented a set of theoretical categories which could not engage with 1938 and its many meanings.

Alternatives and Conclusions

text; my focus here is on writers in the postcolonial moment.

Two major Caribbean thinkers have addressed the need for a historiographic practice organized around subaltern speech and practice: Sylvia Wynter and Walter Rodney (see Wynter 2009, 2010).[10]

11 I pointed this out in an earlier work in which I call for a 'Dread History', one in which 'there should be attempts to excavate from the practices and ideas of subaltern resistance movements in the Caribbean a worldview in which hope is rooted in a conception of the bourgeois colonial world turned upside down and in radical desire'. Although this form of history is in part inspired by the work of Indian subaltern studies, it does not seek to explain Jamaican nationalism nor the failures of constitutional decolonization, but rather seeks to grapple with a kind of historical practice of the Caribbean subaltern in which there are attempts to practise alternative forms of politics and deploy different conceptions of history and historical time than what is conventionally reviewed. In such a project memory is closely allied to historical thought and functions as anamnesis. See Bogues (2003: 179 & 205, note 15).

Writing in the *Jamaica Journal*, Sylvia Wynter observes, 'The history of the Caribbean Islands is in large part the indigenization of the black man. And this history is a cultural history – not in "writing" but of those *homumculi* who humanize the landscape by peopling it with gods and sprits, with demons and duppies, with all the panoply of man's imagination' (1969: 35). Thus, I would argue, any radical historical analysis of the 1938 event would have to think about how this cultural history shaped the actions of those subalterns who shook British colonial power in May-June 1938. The lack of attention to this panoply of the subalterns' imagination is to my mind still a lacuna in historical interpretations of the 1938 events.[11]

Writing in the conclusion of his *History of the Guyanese Working People*, Rodney notes:

This study has sought to show some of the ways in which the Guyanese working class constituted itself through its own activities. Much more will have to be researched and written on the emergence of the culture of working people ... only the opening of a culture history can definitively indicate what made the working people exercise particular choices at given moments: what made them long-suffering or impatient or what transformed them from apathy to combat. (Rodney 1981: 220)

It is sufficient for this essay to note Rodney's preoccupation about how we can write about working people constituting themselves. It is interesting to note that he writes this while he is fully engaged as a political radical in Guyana.

We are well aware that historical events only assume some meaning once they have passed. But how might we understand an event which has been a revolution or a major uprising, a rupture from the everyday? Hannah Arendt makes the point that modern revolutions are 'inextricably bound up with the notion that the course of history suddenly begins anew, that an entirely new story, a story never known or told before is about to unfold' (Arendt 1963: 28). For Arendt, one major difficulty with the modern revolution was the appearance of the social. However, to my mind, it is precisely the appearance of the social in which the question of equality assumes broad proportions. When the social appears it bursts conventional norms, touches and then embraces issues of social justice, new forms of association and economic equality. When this happens the most profound questions about the conditions under which a certain kind of freedom can be exercised are raised. Because revolutions are about new beginnings and an irruption into the everyday, they have a relationship to the future – one not yet known but desired – and to the past because they draw upon memories. Revolutions therefore involve conceptions of historical time. As Walter Benjamin notes, revolution 'blasts open the continuum of history'. I would contend that mass uprisings also disrupt history but, instead of new beginnings, mass uprisings shift old ground and often set new markers. This happens, however, within the frame of continued domination, which is why hegemony is so fluid. Michel de Certeau makes the point that essential to history is the 'description of events, how they are considered meaningful, how they become worthy of notice' (de Certeau 1988: xv). It is the eye which determines what is worthy, and that eye is shaped by many things. It is in the determinations of these shapings that politics resides. In the Jamaican case, the 1938 events were mined for many purposes *but not for the ideas of those who participated in the uprising.*

An attendant difficulty in writing radical Caribbean history is thus that of the archive.[12] In this regard it is important to ponder the recent oral histories about the 1938 events and to recall the ways in which those who participated in the event saw its meaning. For example, Stennet Kerr Coombs, recalling the event and its meanings, observes, 'Since 1938 dem have more respect fi black people. From that time better wages' (Bryan and Watson 2003: 25).[13] Another voice remembers: 'I wouldn't sey I take part in de strike but I wasn't working dere at dat time, but I was in agreement fe di strike. People wanted land to cultivate' (106–7). From these voices I would argue that three elements were central to the consciousness of the rebels in May-June 1938: respect for the black population, which meant the end of racial domination in the colony, better wages and land. All three were summarized in the petition of the Poor Man's Improvement Land Settlement and Labour Association, which serves as an epigraph for this essay (Hill and Small 1974). These demands represented not a revolutionary consciousness in general but a historically specific one, focused on rupturing elements of British colonial rule in the Jamaican colony.

For any rupture to occur within the social requires – in the words of the French historian Jules Michelet – 'for the people to appear'. This is an appearance in which voice and speech merge with action. From this stance one cannot judge an event as a failed revolution or uprising unless we have been able to recompose the contours of 'the thought from below'. This recomposition was what was missing from the popular accounts which we have examined.

Paradoxically, thirty years from the events of 1938, popular histories were being written without much attention to the thought of the actors who made the event. Today, within Caribbean radical historiography, we have not yet answered the question of how we can write a history of ruptural events. How do we write a history in which speakers and actors act not as agents for a theory of revolution or rebellion, but deliver speech and action within the framework of a complex set of historical specificities which, to invoke Walter Benjamin, can be called their own 'tradition/s of the oppressed'? I suggest that this is not a question only about historical knowledge, nor

12 One superb text which successfully produces historical knowledge by thinking about what may be loosely called cultural history is *Neither Led Nor Driven* (Moore and Johnson 2004).

13 The Social History Project is a very important one since it allows new archives to be opened up and we can hear/ listen to subaltern voices.

simply one about a politics of knowledge, but rather one about the very category of the political and the issues which circle around human beings' attempt to reformulate the grounds of an associative community. The 1938 event was one attempt to redraw the boundaries of association within a specific colony. That the event produced unions and parties which are today major elements of Jamaican politics does not mean that the event marked the beginnings of Jamaican political modernity. Rather, it may mean that similar to all social and political events of rupture, there resides within an event itself the possibility of many results. The critical historian recomposes and reconstructs not just to recount what happened but to open ways in which we may interpret what *has* happened. It means working through the articulations of any specific moment. In the case of 1938, it meant grappling with specific forms of consciousness which made the 1938 events possible, and therefore with new archives. That in the 1970s we were not able to do this speaks volumes about our own political understanding of revolution. That today we still take for granted the conventional interpretations of 1938 is indicative of the present political moment in the Caribbean.

References

Arendt, H. (1963) *On Revolution*, London: Penguin.

Augier, R. (ed.) (2008) 'West Indian history', *Caribbean Quarterly* 54 (4).

Augier, R. and Gordon, S. (1962) *Sources of West Indian History*, London: Longmans.

Bogues, A. (ed.) (1998) 'Aspects of Caribbean intellectual tradition', *Small Axe* (September): 140.

Bogues, A. (2002) 'Nationalism and Jamaican political thought', in K. Monteith and G. Richards (eds) *Jamaica in Slavery and Freedom: History, Heritage and Culture*, Kingston: Universtiy of the West Indies Press, pp. 363–87.

Bogues, A. (2003) *Black Heretics, Black Prophets: Radical Political Intellectuals*, New York: Routledge.

Bogues, A. (2010) 'The *Abeng* newspaper: the radical politics of post-colonial blackness' in *Caribbean Thought: History, Literature and Politics*, Princeton: Markus Wiener.

Bolland, O. N. (2001) *The Politics of Labour in the British Caribbean*, Kingston: Ian Randle Press.

Bryan, P. and Watson, K. (2003) *Not for Wages Alone: Eyewitness Summaries of the 1938 Labour Rebellion in Jamaica*, Mona: Department of History, Social History Project, p. 25.

de Certeau, M. (1988) *The Writing of History*, New York: Columbia University Press.

Eaton, G. (1975) *Alexander Bustamante and Modern Jamaica*, Kingston: Kingston Publishers.

Girvan, N. and Meeks, B. (eds) (2010) *The Thought of New World Group*, Kingston: Ian Randle Press.

Hart, R. (1972) [1952] *The Origin and Development of the People of Jamaica*, Montreal: International Caribbean Service Bureau.

Hart, R. (1980) *Slaves Who Abolished Slavery*, Vol. 1, Kingston: Institute of Social and Economic Research, UWI Mona.

Hart, R. (2004) *Time for a Change*, Kingston: Arawak Publishers.

Higman, B. (1999) *Writing West Indian Histories*, London: Macmillian.

Hill, R. and Small, R. (1974) 'The teaching of Robert E. Rumble, A Jamaican peasant leader' in Institute of the Black World (ed.) 'Education and the Black Struggle', special issue of *Harvard Educational Review*.

Lamming, G. and Paquet, S. P. (2001) *In the Castle of My Skin*, Ann Arbor: University of Michigan Press.

Lewis, A. (1977) [1939] *Labour in the West Indies: The Birth of a Workers' Movement*, London: New Beacon Books.

Lewis, R. (1998) *Walter Rodney's Intellectual and Political Thought*, Kingston: University of the West Indies Press.

Moore, B. L. and Johnson, M. A. (2004) *Neither Led Nor Driven: Contesting British Cultural Imperialism in Jamaica, 1865–1920*, Kingston: University of the West Indies Press.

Munroe, T. (1977) *The Marxist Left in Jamaica, 1940–1950*, Kingston: Institute of Social and Economic Research, UWI Mona.

Post, K. (1969) 'The politics of protest in Jamaica, 1938: some problems of analysis and conceptualization", *Social and Economic Studies* 18(4): 374–90.

Post, K. (1978) *Arise Ye Starvelings*, The Hague: Martinus Nijhoff.

Robotham, D. (1975) *Our Struggles*, Kingston: Workers' Liberation League.

Rodney, W. (1981) *A History of the Guyanese Working People, 1881–1905*, Baltimore: Johns Hopkins University Press.

Scott, D. (1998) 'No saviour from high', interview with Ken Post', *Small Axe* 4: 85–157.

Wynter, S. (1969) 'Jonkonnu in Jamaica: towards the interpretation of the folk dance as a cultural process", *Jamaica Journal* 3(4): 35.

Wynter, S. (2009) *Hills of Hebron*, Kingston: Ian Randle Press.

Wynter, S. (2010) *We Must Sit Down and Talk About a Little Culture*, London: Peepal Press.

REVOLUTIONARY PRAXIS IN A POST-NEOLIBERAL ERA

Media Associations and the New Coalitional Politics in Venezuela

Sujatha Fernandes

City University of New York, USA

This essay will look at the new modes of revolutionary praxis evolving in post-neoliberal Venezuela. In particular, it will explore the experiences of media associations such as the Asociación Nacional de Medios Comunitarios, Libres y Alternativos (ANMCLA) in creating broad-based coalitions to interface with the radical government of Hugo Chávez. These coalitions have helped to defend the interests of social movements in their interactions with the Chávez government, which has carried out substantial anti-neoliberal policies but remains subject to the constraints of global capital. This form of coalitional politics is distinct from the trade unions and mass organizations that were the vehicles for radical politics during the Cuban Revolution. The changing face of radical politics reflects both the changing terrain of struggle as a result of neoliberal hegemony, but also an attempt to come to terms with legacies of authoritarianism in the Left.

This essay explores the new modes of revolutionary praxis emerging in contemporary Venezuela, and looks at how social movements have been able to create sustainable structures of representation and accountability in a post-neoliberal era. Social movements began to gather pace in Venezuela during the 1990s alongside the appearance and consequent election of the radical leader Hugo Chávez. Chávez implemented a series of anti-neoliberal and pro-poor measures that dramatically changed the course of the country, but at the same time, his administration remains subject to the constraints of global capital. This contradiction has been most apparent as the Chávez government searches for foreign investment, introducing market-based logics in certain demarcated zones. The crisis came to a fore with the government's plan to increase coal mining in Zulia with the aid of multinational companies, undermining the livelihoods of indigenous people in the area and subjecting them to a toxic environment. The slippage between the revolutionary rhetoric of the state and the reality of its continued accommodation of foreign investors produced criticisms from social movements, who organized protests. In this essay, I explore the coalitions that are being built from the ground up, and I evaluate their potential to function as institutional linkages in the contemporary period.

Some scholars have argued that functioning institutional channels between state and society depend on a strong procedural democracy. Procedural democracy, derived from western experiences of representative government, is based on the rule of law, free and fair elections, and a separation of powers between the executive, legislative, and the judicial branches of government. The changes carried out by Chávez during his administration have provoked concern among some political scientists and western-based human rights organizations that this procedural democracy is being eroded. Javier Corrales (2005: 107) argues that the new Constitution, which was approved by popular referendum in December 1999, expanded the executive branch at the expense of the other branches by concentrating power in the presidency. According to Jennifer McCoy (2004: 279–81), since Chávez has been in power he has systematically attacked institutional structures by intervening in the court system through the constituent assembly and disbarring several judges, appointing Supreme Court members by decree, and increasing the power of the military by removing congressional oversight over military promotions. And in 2004, critics such as Human Rights Watch add, Chávez carried out actions to control Venezuela's judicial branch by increasing the size of the Supreme Court from 20 to 32 members, thereby further undercutting the separation of powers and undermining the rule of law.[1] Although some observers have refuted these claims,[2] most assessments of the Chávez government from outside continue to be based in the language of procedural democracy.

Yet in criticisms coming from urban social movements, this explicit focus on procedural democracy is a limited means of ensuring government accountability and institutional mediation, as it reduces citizen participation

1 Testimony of José Miguel Vivanco, Executive Director Americas Division, Human Rights Watch, Washington, DC, June 24, 2004, online at www.hrw.org/english/docs/2004/07/07/venezu9020.htm.

2 See Grandin (2007), who argues that the legislation had provided numerous mechanisms for debate over these actions, and furthermore they were justified because the court had failed to absolve military officers involved in the 2002 coup and the measures were essential to fulfilling the social mandate of the government.

to elections once every six years. Fernando Pinto, a young media activist, explained to me that, moreover, it removes decision-making power from the people: 'What liberal democracy has done is separate who decides from who votes: you vote, but you lose the real capacity to decide about the things that affect you.' In contrast to the focus among some with procedural democracy, urban social movements in Venezuela are concerned with *substantive* democracy, defined by John and Jean Comaroff (1997: 141) as 'a civic culture in which participatory politics would be the stuff of everyday life'. While procedural democracy relies on multi-party elections as a means of ensuring accountability, and trusts in branches of government to monitor each other as the principle of separation of powers, others have spoken about the need for social accountability that counts on social movements and organizations to monitor the government (Smulovitz and Peruzzotti 2000, 2006). Social movement activists have expressed concerns about a concentration of power in the figure of the presidency, but unlike the adherents of procedural democracy, they propose an accountability from below as a means of counterbalancing that power.

Modes of Political Organization in Cuba and Venezuela

The Bolivarian Revolution in Venezuela diverges from earlier revolutionary projects in the region such as the Cuban Revolution because of its own unique characteristics, but also because of the changed circumstances of global capitalism. In the 1960s, the existence of the Soviet Union created a counter to the geopolitical influence of the United States, providing assistance to revolutionary and decolonizing nations that wanted to remain outside the orbit of the western superpower. Import substitution industrialization (ISI) policies in vogue across Latin America and most of the Third World emphasized nationalization of the export sector with the objective of strengthening capital accumulation. This led to large working classes organized in trade unions and parties who formed a strong institutional basis for populist, revolutionary and nationalist leaderships. At the same time, the large base of impoverished poor in the countryside bolstered armed strategies of rural guerrilla warfare that helped leaders like Che Guevara and Fidel Castro to build a mass following.

By the period of the 1990s, a new global order was being consolidated. The Soviet Union had collapsed and in its place emerged a unipolar system dominated by the United States. Neoliberal policies of deregulation, privatization and free trade were being imposed by multilateral lending agencies. Globalization and deindustrialization fragmented the working class and drove unemployed workers into a burgeoning yet precarious informal sector. Revolutionary movements across the region seemed to be in retreat. In 1990 the Frente Sandinista de Liberación Nacional (FSLN) was voted out of office in Nicaragua, after years of a devastating economic embargo and war sponsored by the United States. Cuba entered a severe economic crisis as a result of the decline in Soviet aid and export income, and was forced to re-enter the global market. Neoliberal policies were adopted by parties as diverse as the Peronist Party in Argentina, the Socialist Party of Chile, and the Partido Revolucionario Institucional (PRI) in Mexico.

The contemporary reemergence of the revolutionary Left is partly due to the exclusions and failures of the new global order. But this new stage of capitalism, where production and accumulation have been globalized, has also made it harder for individual nations to sustain independent polities and economies. As leaders such as Chávez and Evo Morales in Bolivia mount challenges to the neoliberal paradigm, their economies remain subject to the constraints of global capital. The Venezuelan economy continues to be dependent on a boom-bust cycle of fluctuating oil rents and an export-oriented model of development. At the same time, the Chávez government's policies of land and resource redistribution, social welfare intervention, and restructuring of trade to promote joint ventures and 'fair trade' bilateral agreements are incompatible with a neoliberal agenda. As the financial resources and influence of the International Monetary Fund (IMF) have entered into decline, Venezuela has offered alternative sources of credit to countries like Argentina to pay off their debt, as well as giving loans and oil subsidies to other countries in the region, without the conditions imposed by the IMF.

The changed conditions for revolutionary practice in the twenty-first century have led to new kinds of political organization and models of collectivity. In an earlier era of mass politics, parties and trade unions were able to reach and represent large constituencies, they had an impact on policymaking at various levels, and they were able to build national and international alliances to support workers' struggles. But over time, many of these structures have become rigid and unresponsive to the demands of their constituencies. Given the greater informalization of the workforce; the growing importance of ethnicity, race and gender; and the shift away from the factory to the barrio as the site of labour and social life, traditional political parties and trade unions have proven to be outdated and inflexible. New forms of worker struggle have been emerging through the recuperated factory movement, landless workers movement, and independent workers centres, which recognize the changed conditions of labour under neoliberalism. Like other innovative revolutionary social movements such as community based radio and indigenous movements, these forms of struggle emphasize democratic participation through popular assembly and strategic alliances with the state that allow them to retain their independence. Yet while social movements maintain a degree of autonomy through their local organizing work in community spaces, they are always vulnerable to directed mobilization from above and the institutionalization of their struggles.

State-Society Links under Chávez: The Formation of ANMCLA

Contemporary Venezuela under Chávez has been characterized by growing popular activism and a simultaneous concentration of power in the figure of Chávez. Since his first public appearances during his attempted coups of 1992, Chávez had established a strong personal connection with the masses, but he has been less successful in creating enduring institutions that could mediate the relationship between state and society. The Chávez government attempted to build the links between state and society through a series of methods. Initially, the government strengthened Chávez's party, the Movimiento Quinta Republica (MVR), thinking that it would be the main vehicle for state-society interactions. For his first year in government, Chávez operated solely through the party, and most non-party activity was not considered important. However, the MVR proved to be bureaucratic, hierarchical and removed from the lives of ordinary people. The MVR was originally conceived as an electoral front controlled by Chávez's clandestine cell, the Movimiento Bolivariano Revolucionario 200 (MBR-200). Since the founders of the MVR did not consider it to be a party, they did not create democratic procedures for internal debate. The hierarchical structure of the party consisted of Bolivarian coordinators at the municipal and regional level, and a national directorate with decision-making power, consisting of civilian and former military leaders. Yet the electoral successes of the organization thrust it into the spotlight and gradually reduced the significance of the MBR-200 (López Maya 2003: 80–3). The MVR frequently attempted to intervene in local initiatives, mobilize the base in support of various electoral initiatives, and absorb independent expressions into its fold.

Given the failures of the MVR, Chávez then tried to promote local units of participation such as the Círculos Bolivarianos (CBs) and between 2001 and 2003 there were around 200,000 CBs formed across the country. However, according to its own members, the CBs collapsed due to 'incapacity, neglect, exhaustion, and evolution' (Botía 2005). In their place, new structures were created such as the Unidades de Batalla Electoral (Units of Electoral Battle, UBEs), which successfully organized people to defend Chávez in the referendum of 2004. After the referendum, these were converted into the Unidades de Batalla Social (Units of Social Battle, UBSs). As community media activist Carlos Lugo described it, while the CBs, UBEs and UBSs originally facilitated popular participation, they were eventually taken over by political parties and institutions, and the transference of power to the local level that some groups hoped for did not happen.

Chávez also attempted to bypass the traditional institutions, with their high levels of corruption, by creating the Missions, which sought to channel resources directly to the community. The Missions did have some success in avoiding the bureaucracy of the institutions. For example, in the Barrio Adentro programme of local health clinics, people in the barrios arranged to find housing for Cuban doctors, and they themselves supervised the health modules. Likewise, with the soup kitchens, resources arrive directly from the government, without the red tape of the Health and Social Welfare and Social Security institutions. At times, however, the Missions reproduce the paternalism, corruption and hierarchy of the institutions. The Universidad Bolivariana de Venezuela (Bolivarian University of Venezuela, UBV) is a case in point. At one point, a small faction took over control of the UBV and began to use undemocratic methods in its running, excluding the teachers and students from decisions-making. They would call for *asambleas informativas* (informative assemblies) to advise the teachers about the direction of the institution, and in their frustration of being left out of decision-making, several teachers resigned. The continuing hegemony of a vanguardist logic in attempts to organize popular movements from above resulted in growing disillusionment with these methods.

In this context, media associations have provided an important vehicle for uniting diverse social movements and allowing them to interface with the state. Given the growth of communications technology, and the changing sites of working-class politics from the factory to the barrio, it is not surprising that barrio-based media associations should play a role in building a coalitional politics. Radio, especially, has functioned as an organizing nucleus for diverse committees and movements in the barrio. The media association that has been most concerned with building alliances among urban social movements is the Asociación Nacional de Medios Comunitarios, Libres y Alternativos (ANMCLA). ANMCLA has its roots in a loose network of radio producers, known as Banda Ciudadana, formed in 1992. According to Fernando Pinto, the idea of the network emerged during the social explosions of the early 1990s, as a means of communicating what was happening on the ground during the coups of 1992 and beyond. The group gave workshops on radio to people in Catia, Caricuao and La Vega, helping to start the radios in those areas. After Chávez was elected in 1998, the activists from Banda Ciudadana realized that they needed to unify their forces and build a more coherent organization.

Media activists began meeting in 2001 to discuss the idea of creating an organization, and in 2002 they formed ANMCLA. Prior to the opposition's attempted coup against Chávez in 2002, the group had been mostly an idea; as most of the members were involved in their own individual collectives and community organizations, the broader grouping had little resonance. It was only after the coup of 2002 that ANMCLA began to function as an organization. In December 2003 they held a conference in the northwestern Andean town of Mérida, uniting media collectives from across the country. There were certain aspects of the organization that were agreed on from the start: that ANMCLA was not a party or a union, but a social movement; that it had to function as a way of integrating all their struggles, not only in the area of communication; they had to work to multiply the media in the hands of popular sectors; and lastly, they had to connect with all of the long-term social movements that pre-dated Chávez and help them to create community media. It was by connecting with these long-term groups, especially in rural areas such as Yaracuy and Zulia, that ANMCLA grew so rapidly, says Fernando Pinto. The organization integrated movements of urban barrio communities with indigenous movements, the miners' struggle, and the peasant movements.

The founders of ANMCLA were concerned that social movements needed a national organization that would allow them to counter the centralization of power in the private media, in the state and in corporations. ANMCLA as an organization has engaged in several kinds of protest and deliberative activities as a way of realizing their vision of a substantive democracy. One form of action, connected with the resignification of public space, is marches and mobilizations. During the tense days of the work stoppage by oil executives from the state-owned oil company PDVSA in December 2001, both Chávez's supporters and the opposition would take regularly to the streets. This was important, as Fernando Pinto notes, as 'all the heavy political events, at least in Venezuela, have been lived in the street'. But in 2005, ANMCLA began calling marches in defence of the interests of its members, such as mobilizations against the Chávez government's plan to increase coal mining in the state of Zulia.

'In defence of water and life': Strategies of Mobilization

When Chávez was elected to government, he adopted many of the contracts to mining companies that had been granted under previous governments. But following the restructuring of the oil industry in 2003 to promote joint ventures where the state has majority ownership, the Chávez government made efforts to develop state control over key sectors such as bauxite, iron and coal. In the southeast state of Guyana, where the majority of the country's mines, hydroelectricity capacity and steel works are located, the state is revising mining concessions to also move toward joint ventures. Gregory Albo (2006: 7–8) argues that in a hostile global context, the ability of Venezuela to diversify depends on planning capacities at the centre and the development of independent capacities in new agencies, but old state structures have been a significant obstacle to this. And although the state is attempting to control the significant natural resources of the country and restrict the license of multi-national companies to exploit these resources, its broader strategy remains based upon an export-oriented model of development where those who profit from and consume resources are still mostly foreign corporations and citizens. These contradictions came to the fore with the proposal of the Chávez government to increase coal mining in the state of Zulia.

In October 2004, just months before signing a trade agreement with Cuba under the auspices of an anti-neoliberal, pro-sustainable development model known as ALBA (Alternativa Bolivariana para las Américas), the Chávez government announced plans to increase coal mining in Zulia. Venezuela extracts 8.5 million metric tons of coal per year, which is predominantly for export to the United States and Europe.[3] Around 80 per cent of this coal comes from two mines located north of the Manuelote water reservoir in Zulia, the Mina Norte and the Mina Paso Diablo. These mines are controlled by joint ventures with private consortia where the government is a minority partner. Extensive coal mining in these locations has already displaced local indigenous people. In 2004, Corpozulia, the regional development corpora-tion of the national government, planned to open coal mines along the Cachirí and Socuy rivers to increase extraction of coal from 8,000 tons to 30,000 tons. Maracaibo, the capital of Zulia, home to over two and a half million people, is dependent on the sources of water that come from these two rivers. The government plan to increase production involved the investment of hundreds of millions of dollars for the construction of a megaport for the extraction and transport of coal by multinationals. Corpozulia also planned to build a thermo-electric plant of 500 megawatts, fuelled by coal to supply electricity to the state.[4] The indigenous Wayuu, Barí and Yukpa people from the area were concerned that the plans would increase water contamination and health risks for the mostly indigenous population of the region who depend on scarce water supplies. They argued that the proposal violated the Kyoto Agreement and several articles of the Bolivarian Constitution that guarantee a clean environment and protection of indigenous resources.

In March 2005 and January 2006, ANMCLA brought together urban media activists with indigenous groups in mobilizations in Caracas to protest against the plans. On 31 March 2005 a group including over six hundred indigenous people marched from the Plaza Morelos to the Miraflores Presidential Palace. They presented a letter of protest to Chávez, noting the illnesses suffered by mining workers, the threat to the water supply, and the accidents occurring during the transport of coal.[5] Like the Water Wars in Bolivia, the protesters focused on protecting customary usage (Laurie, Andolina and Radcliffe 2002). In a statement to the press, the activists claimed that the extraction of coal constitutes a violation of the rights of the indigenous people 'whose culture and mode of life are absolutely connected with nature'. Posters at the march read: 'Coal Miners of Maché, Socuy, and

3 See
www.stocks.us.
reuters.com/stocks/
fullDescription.
asp?symbol=BTU&
WTmodLOC=
C5–Profile-1
(accessed 23April
2008).

4 Robin Nieto, 'El
costo ambiental de la
explotación del
carbón en
Venezuela', online at
www.voltairenet.
org/article123213.
html.

5 Sarah Wagner,
'Venezuela's
indigenous protest
against coal mining
in their lands', online
at www.venezuel
analysis.com/news.
php?newsno=1569.

Yachirá Out: In defense of water!' and 'No to Coal, Yes to life and nature'. The indigenous protesters wore traditional outfits, including grass skirts, beads, painted faces, and woven baskets on their heads, and many of the women were bare chested. They emphasized their identity as indigenous people, as a way of staking claim to water as a resource that belongs to them as a collective right. In contrast to a development model based on large-scale industrial projects and modernist ideals of progress, the protesters emphasized Andean cosmologies and the defence of their cultural heritage as indigenous people.

The urban protesters who joined the indigenous people on the march similarly drew on the language of Andean spirituality and cultural heritage. The march was a dramatic expression of the ways that the urban poor deploy indigenous identity as a means of framing their resistance. As Nancy Postero (2007: 195) has argued in the context of Bolivia, this is not simply a strategic use of indigenous identity, but rather 'a new form of coalitional politics that is emerging as the most important form of social movement protagonism'. Although many of the protesters in the march were indigenous or, in the case of the urban poor, with some mixture of indigenous background, they did not mobilize as indigenous people, but rather they united around a common sense of exclusion. The number of indigenous groups directly affected by the mining plan was very small, some fifty households or so, which makes this kind of coalitional politics even more important to make their voices heard nationally.

The protesters took on the language and symbols of the Chávez government itself, to challenge its plans for coal mining. In the press statement, they cite principles of environmental protection (Article 129), individual and collective rights to quality of life (Article 127), the role of the state to guarantee a contamination-free environment (Article 127), and maintaining the cultural, social and economic integrity of indigenous groups (Article 120), that are being violated by the plan to increase coal mining. Drawing on the language of popular protagonism framed within the Bolivarian Constitution, the protesters argued that the mining constitutes 'a violation of the right to participation and the democratic principle of popular protagonism'. In both the 31 March and 27 January marches, the 'No to Coal' signs used the 'No' symbol of the pro-Chávez campaigners during the recall referendum, as a way of signalling the ways they have supported Chávez, who must now live up to his promises. Protesters carried signs with slogans such as 'Venezuela: Now it is for everyone' and 'There is no fatherland without us', appealing to the official mottos of inclusiveness being touted by the government. The signs referred to Chávez as *compañero*, and many of the protesters said that they had come because they wanted Chávez to know what was going on in Zulia.

At the same time, the protesters were highly critical of the model of development represented by the coal mining, and by extension, that undergirds the Bolivarian project. In their press statement they said, 'The plans for coal mining in Zulia are part of an exogenous strategy that weaken self-determination, and moreover, are in keeping with a hegemonic economic and productive model in the world, that identifies development with economic expansion and a growth in the consumption of energy.' One of the posters at the march had an image of the Grim Reaper, draped in the American flag, which read, 'Exploiting coal is death!!! And money for transnationals.' In contrast to the government slogan, 'Another world is possible', the protesters claim, 'Another integration is possible'. Social movements in the barrios have long been engaged in struggles again contamination and pollution, and some see the Chávez government as no different to its predecessors regarding environmental policy. Government propaganda declares that PDVSA has been reclaimed from multinational corporations and now belongs to the people, in slogans such as 'PDVSA: Now it is for Everyone'. To some degree, government rhetoric has associated an improvement in standards of living of the urban poor with greater exploitation of natural resources.

The march raised the question of what democracy looks like and who makes decisions in a democracy. In the press release, the protesters state that Article 120 of the Constitution gives indigenous people the right to participate in decision-making in issues regarding their social, economic and cultural integrity, but in the case of the mining the decisions are being made by the authorities in collaboration with transnational companies. Rusbel Palmar, a leader of a Zulia indigenous organization, said, 'The coal infrastructure plans have not been presented to indigenous people. These plans cannot be done without consultation with indigenous people.'[6] The government decision highlighted the lack of accountability of officials to their constituents. The press release states: 'The majority of sectors of the Yukpa, Barí and Wayuu people, among the others affected, reject the projects for the exploitation of coal, and that their voice is not being adequately heard by the authorities, which constitutes a violation of the right to participation and the democratic principle of popular protagonism.' By mobilizing in the street, the people are not just protesting against the government's plans, they are also shaping a new vision of what substantive democracy should look like. As the people organized, they created alternative structures of decision-making and social power that challenged the monopoly of the state and transnational corporations.

Through mobilizations, protesters also reclaim the streets as the site of politics, and a space for renewing local power. In contrast to the large marches of 300,000 and 500,000 people supporting Chávez during the oil strikes of 2001, after the referendum people began to mobilize autonomously. The marches had some degree of success in raising popular awareness

6 Cited in Nieto, 'El costo ambiental'.

about environmental concerns, and also in halting the plans. After the 31 March protest, the government ordered two commissions, which found that the protesters were correct about the contaminating impact of the mining. The ministry of the environment and another special commission in Miraflores issued statements and reports supporting these findings. But the government has not acted strongly on these findings. As of May 2006, they had postponed their plans to increase coal mining to 30,000 tons, leaving it at 8,000 tons, but they had not met protesters' demands to reduce it to zero. The protesters think that the government will continue pushing for the increase in production, which requires them to be vigilant and ready to take to the streets. ANMCLA has played a crucial mediating role in organizing the marches, building coalitions between rural and urban sectors, and providing a common platform for groups seeking more autonomy. Nevertheless, there is still further important coalition-building work to reach out to and involve mining workers, who have been pitted against indigenous groups by mining corporations.

Conclusion

In the contemporary period, we can see the emergence of new sites of social struggle, novel forms of collectivity, and different relationships being forged between society and state. Building a new form of coalitional politics has become the most urgent task facing fragmented social movements. These coalitions have been particularly important in the case of the campaigns against coal mining, where the affected indigenous groups are small in numbers. Urban and rural groups succeeded in constructing a broader front to protest the issue of coal mining, linking it to an analysis and critique of modernizing development.

Within this new coalitional politics, questions of democracy have come to the fore. Barrio-based media activists from Caracas, indigenous groups and others are concerned with substantive democracy that gives them the ability to have decision-making powers over the issues that affect them. Democracy was to be realized through mobilizations in the streets, occupations of state institutions, and regular assemblies. The activists from ANMCLA sought to redefine the meaning of participation, as more than government-sponsored rallies that mobilized people in support of the state, but as the building of self-generating and autonomous movements.

One of the core issues that activists confront is the degree of agency they can retain within a state-led process of transformation. In addition to strategies of direct action, they have pursued diverse paths outside of state institutions, as a way to build their movement without being isolated. Making transnational alliances is an important part of the new coalitional politics – forging regional links not just from the state, but from the grassroots. While the Chávez government has proposed an alternative trade agreement, the Bolivarian Alternative for the Americas (ALBA), ANMCLA and others have sought to organize grassroots exchanges such as regional meetings of social movements and community based media. Although a discussion of transnationalism is beyond the scope of this essay, there is no question that transnational exchanges are going to play a crucial role in bolstering social movements as part of the processes of radical change taking place across the Americas. Sharing the experiences of grassroots political learning can provide important resources for those who want a greater role for social movements in new revolutionary governments against those who seek to solidify bureaucratic power within state institutions.

Acknowledgement

Some sections of this essay are drawn from my book, *Who Can Stop the Drums? Urban Social Movements in Chávez's Venezuela* (forthcoming, Duke University Press). This research was made possible with the support of faculty research grants from Princeton University and the PSC-CUNY Research Foundation.

References

Albo, G. (2006) 'The unexpected revolution: Venezuela confronts neoliberalism.' Paper presented at the International Development Week, University of Alberta, Canada.

Botía, A. (2005) 'Círculos Bolivarianos Parecen Burbujas en el Limbo', *Últimas Noticias*, 20 March.

Comaroff, J. L. and Comaroff, J. (1997) 'Postcolonial politics and discourses of democracy in Southern Africa: an anthropological reflection on African political modernities', *Journal of Anthropological Research* 53(2): 123–46.

Corrales, J. (2005) 'In search of a theory of polarization: lessons from Venezuela, 1999–2005', *Revista Europea de Estudios Latinoamericanos y del Caribe* 79: 105–118.

Grandin, G. (2007) 'Countervailing powers', *LASA Forum Focus* 28(1): 14–17.

Laurie, N., Andolina, R. and Radcliffe, S. (2002) 'The excluded "indigenous"? The implications of multi-ethnic policies for water reform in Bolivia', in R. Sieder (ed.) *Multiculturalism in Latin America: Indigenous Rights, Diversity, and Democracy*, New York: Palgrave Macmillan, pp. 252–76.

López Maya, M. (2003) 'Hugo Chávez Frías: his movement and his presidency', in S. Ellner and D. Hellinger (eds) *Venezuelan Politics in the Chávez Era: Class, Polarization and Conflict*, Boulder: Lynne Riener, pp. 73–91.

McCoy, J. (2004) 'From representative to participatory democracy? Regime transformation in Venezuela', in J. McCoy and D. Myers (eds) *The Unraveling of Representative Democracy in Venezuela*, Baltimore: Johns Hopkins University Press, pp. 263–95.

Postero, N. G. (2007) *Now We are Citizens: Indigenous Politics in Postmulticultural Bolivia*, Stanford: Stanford University Press.

Smulovitz, C. and Peruzzotti, E. (2000) 'Societal accountability in Latin America', *Journal of Democracy* 11(4): 147–58.

Smulovitz, C. and Peruzzotti, E. (eds) (2006) *Enforcing the Rule of Law: Social Accountability in the New Latin American Democracies*, Pittsburgh: University of Pittsburgh Press.

TECHNIFICATION, SWEETIFICATION, TREATYFICATION

Politics of the Caribbean-EU Economic Partnership Agreement

Norman Girvan

University of the West Indies, Trinidad and Tobago

This essay discusses the lessons to be learnt from the efforts of a Caribbean citizens' coalition to secure review and renegotiation of the Economic Partnership Agreement (EPA) negotiated between 15 Caribbean countries and the European Union in 2008. To this end it examines the roles of ideology, power, governance and politics. It argues that the EPA institutionalizes a relationship of asymmetrical power with the European Union that is based on the principles of neoliberal globalization; and that it was secured through the manipulation of an unequal power relationship buttressed by the use of neoliberal economic theory to provide a cover for commercial motives. In explaining the politics of the EPA, it proposes the existence of a 'Technification-Sweetification-Treatyfication' syndrome. This refers to the use of technical jargon in policy debates in ways that restrict broad political participation in decision-making; to exaggeration of the presumed benefits of the agreement in order to facilitate its political acceptance; and to incorporation of the agreement into a legally binding international treaty in ways that circumscribe present and future government policies. Citizen advocacy on the EPA was further complicated by the amorphous structure of regional governance and by the organizational and ideological weaknesses of the regional progressive movement. These lessons can help to inform the future strategies of Caribbean governments and civil society.

Introduction

In October 2008, fifteen states of the Cariforum group, consisting of 14 Caribbean Community (Caricom) countries and the Dominican Republic, signed an 'Economic Partnership Agreement' (EPA) with the European Union. The EPA will govern EU-Caribbean economic relations in a wide range of subject areas for the indefinite future. The signing came after an intense and divisive public debate arising from the efforts of a citizens' coalition to secure review and renegotiation of the agreement. This essay discusses lessons for the Caribbean progressive movement from the politics of the EPA.

Background

Since 1975, trade relations between Europe and the African, Caribbean and Pacific (ACP) group of countries had been governed by the principle of 'non-reciprocity' enshrined in the Lomé Convention (ACP-EEC 1975). This meant that most ACP exports entered Europe duty free, while import tariffs were levied on goods imported by the ACP from Europe (European Commission 2006a). After the establishment of the World Trade Organization (WTO) in 1995, this arrangement was determined to be contrary to world trade rules (Atarah 1999). In 2000, Lomé was replaced by the EU-ACP Cotonou Partnership Agreement (CPA), which mandated the negotiation of WTO-compatible 'Economic Partnership Agreements' (EPAs) between the EU and the ACP over 2001–7 (ACP-EEC 2000). The EPAs were supposed to facilitate development and poverty reduction in ACP countries. However, the EU brought the EPA negotiations in line with its global trade policy objectives to secure markets, natural resources and investment opportunities in emerging economies (European Commission 2006b; Seattle to Brussels Network 2006). Hence, EU officials defined the 'development dimension' of EPAs to mean liberalization of trade and investment with Europe and inclusion of investor-friendly rules covering subjects such as investment, services, government purchases, competition and intellectual property – subjects that the EU had failed to get included in the WTO agreement because of opposition from developing countries as a whole. The WTO-plus model agreements sought by Europe were diplomatically termed 'Full' EPAs

1 According to Bartels (2008), the December 2007 deadline had been 'manufactured'.

2 A letter of 25 November 2007 from the president of the European Commission to Caricom leaders threatened disruption of their trade with the EU if agreement were not reached within a matter of weeks. In the event, Cariforum was the only group to initial a 'Full' EPA by the December 2007 deadline; 18 other ACP countries initialled 'Interim' EPAs and continued negotiating into 2008 and 2009.

– implying that anything short of the desired model would be an inferior product.

The EPA negotiations pitted one of the largest trading blocs in the world against some of the world's smallest and poorest countries. EU negotiators employed 'divide and conquer' strategies and 'carrot and stick' tactics in which Europe's aid programme and access to the EU market were the principal instruments. The seventy six ACP countries were split into six negotiating groups; and the ACP was further divided by giving the poorest countries duty free access to the EU market in 2001. Countries that resisted European demands were bypassed, splitting the groups even further. The Cariforum group, which agreed at an early stage to negotiate a 'Full' EPA, was promised priority in aid allocations; and their negotiators were flattered. The most effective weapon was the EU threat to impose punitive tariffs on ACP countries that did not conclude EPA negotiations by 31 December 2007. This was a direct breach of an undertaking given in the Cotonou agreement (Stevens 2007) and the legal basis has been critiqued (Bartels 2007, 2008).[1] But it was a decisive factor in securing agreement by Caricom leaders to key European demands on the EPA text that was initialled just two weeks before the deadline.[2] Thus, the EU 'had "worked" a monumental deception on the region', 'through a mixture of blatant bullyism, bribery, cajolery, deception, intellectual dishonesty and plain bluff' (Thomas 2008a).

Caribbean EPA Protests, 2008

3 The summary which follows draws on the numerous documents related to the Cariforum EPA on the website of the CRNM (www.crnm.org) and at www.normangir van.info/Cariforum-ec-economic-partnership-agreement-epa/, including the 'open letter' to Caricom heads by Havelock Brewster and others; statements by 'concerned citizens', the Caribbean Policy Development Centre (CPDC), and the

During most of the period of the Cariforum EPA negotiations (2004–7) the subject received very limited attention from the media and the wider public. NGOs had organized anti-EPA demonstrations in some Caricom countries in 2004, but these were relatively small and were not sustained. The major part of the EPA controversy took place between finalization of the negotiations in November-December 2007 and ministerial signature of the EPA in October 2008. Critics included at least one head of government, senior academics, former senior Caribbean officials, civil society representatives, labour unions, several parliamentary opposition parties, media commentators and several international NGOs, think tanks and experts.[3] Defenders included the Caribbean negotiators (officials of the Caribbean Regional Negotiating Machinery – CRNM), heads and ministers of regional governments, other government officials, export industry representatives, media commentators and senior European Commission officials. The controversy marked an acrimonious public fracturing of elite consensus on the direction of Caricom's future development and the nature of its international economic relations.

Caribbean Labour Congress (CLC); papers by Havelock Brewster, Norman Girvan, Vaughan Lewis and Clive Thomas, and media articles and reports on statements by Dennis Pantin, Prime Minister Bruce Golding, President Bharrat Jagdeo, Sir Shridath Ramphal, Sir Ronald Sanders, Rickey Singh and other newspaper commentaries posted at www.normangir van.info/epa-in-the-media.

4 The EU market was opened for 29 categories of services exports for firms and 11 categories for self-employed professionals – said to be unprecedented in the WTO and in the EU's bilateral agreements.

The issues concerned both process and content. Critics argued that given the wide scope, legally binding nature and indefinite duration of the EPA there had been inadequate information provided and insufficient opportunities for public input. They called for more public education and consultation and additional time for public review, and, if necessary, renegotiation. The CRNM showed where national consultative committees had been formed and industry consultative groups had been established and enumerated the meetings held. They documented the information provided to governments and the approval secured for negotiating positions. They argued that it would be unwise and impractical to reopen the initialled text for renegotiation, as Cariforum could end up with a less advantageous agreement.

Regarding content, the CRNM and several government leaders insisted that the EPA was the best deal possible under the circumstances. It had 'locked in' duty free quota free (DFQF) access to the EU market, while securing permanent exclusion from duty free treatment of thirteen per cent of Cariforum imports from Europe, with an extended period of liberalization lasting up to twenty five years for the remainder. It had opened up substantial opportunities for services exports to Europe, which was vital to the Caribbean's future economic development.[4] It had a strong 'development dimension', with provisions for development cooperation inserted throughout the text. Cariforum, by being the first to sign a 'Full' EPA, would be well placed to access funding under the EU's Aid for Trade programme. The EPA would support regional integration by bringing the Dominican Republic into a common regime with Caricom in trade in goods and services, movement of capital, and 'trade-related policies' and would boost completion of the Caricom Single Market and Economy. In addition, several exceptions, safeguards and flexibilities had been built into the agreement to protect Caribbean interests.

On content, the critics argued that the Caribbean had given away too much and secured too little. First, to cope with free trade with Europe, Caribbean economies would need substantial resources to upgrade infra-structure and human resources and local firms would need targeted programmes of technical and financial assistance, synchronized with the import liberalization. But no new funding had been provided under the EPA and the promises of development assistance made in the text were not quantified and not time-bound and were therefore not assured and not legally enforceable. Second, the right of governments to foster the development of local firms would be restricted by rules requiring equality of treatment with European firms. Third, the non-tariff barriers to entering the EU market had not been adequately addressed by the EPA. The force of these barriers was shown by the fact that DFQF access had existed for the majority of Caribbean exports since 1976, but exports of new products had hardly grown. Fourth, the opening of European services markets to the Caribbean would be of limited practical value because of the stringent eligibility requirements.

Fifth, the critics protested that the scope of the EPA went beyond the requirements of WTO rules in ways that would limit future development policies and preempt the rules to be established for Caricom's own integration project, the Caricom Single Market and Economy (CSME). In addition, this would undermine the negotiating position of the ACP and the developing country bloc in the WTO and commit the position of Caricom in future negotiations with other trade partners. Sixth, the EPA would marginalize the CSME and foreclose the strategy of consolidating the regional economy as a platform for engaging with the world economy. Seventh, the EPA's 'Most Favoured Nation Clause' would hinder development of trade relations with emerging economies of the South. Eighth, the 'Regional Preference' clause would eliminate the special treatment granted to Caricom's 'Less Developed Countries' (LDCs, principally the members of the Organization of East Caribbean States – OECS) provided under the Caricom treaty and the Caricom-Dominican Republic Free Trade Agreement. Finally, it was argued that the EPA's implementation machinery contained a degree of supranationality not even present in Caricom's own governance machinery, in that decisions taken by the Joint Cariforum-EC Council are legally binding on the Caricom member states.

The criticisms coalesced into a protest movement/advocacy campaign aimed at (1) postponing the initialling and, later, the signing of the EPA and (2) renegotiating the agreement. In November 2007 four prominent academic and civil society representatives had directed an 'open letter' to Caricom leaders to delay the finalization of negotiations.[5] Shortly after the EPA initialling there was a public split among Caricom governments when President Jagdeo of Guyana contradicted some of his fellow leaders by telling a press conference 'we got nothing from the EPA'. This elicited a stinging rejoinder from Prime Minister Golding of Jamaica, who accused critics of the EPA of 'mendicancy'. But President Jagdeo's statement triggered organization of an online petition by a group of 'concerned citizens' calling for public review of the negotiated text, which attracted support from over 100 academics, civil society leaders, private sector leaders and others within the region and in the Caribbean diaspora. Two regional academics also published critiques of the EPA. The CRNM mounted a vigorous defence of the agreement, portraying their version of the EPA as 'Fact' and that of the critics as 'Fiction'. The CRNM's role in the negotiations was criticized by Caricom trade ministers in January and the Caricom secretariat was tasked with commissioning a review of the process.[6] A lively media debate ensued. In March three of the EPA's most prominent critics publicly petitioned the governments to 'renegotiate the EPA' and to this end proposed a four-pronged

5 There was no official response to this letter.

6 The report of this task force was critical of the lack of effective ministerial oversight of the EPA negotiations and of proper coordination between the CRNM and the Caricom secretariat. One eventual result was that in 2009 the Caricom heads of government decided to abolish the quasi-autonomous status of the CRNM and bring it under the aegis of the Caricom secretariat.

7 (1) Securing additional time for consultation/ evaluation, (2) restricting its scope, (3) proposing 'targeted support' for firms' supply and marketing capabilities, and (4) action to mobilize support from domestic and international constituencies. See 'Renegotiate the EPA' by Havelock Brewster, Norman Girvan and Vaughan Lewis, online at www.normangirvan. info/renegotiate-epa/.

8 Ministerial signing of the EPA was variously reported as scheduled for March, June and July of 2008 (and ultimately October, in order to allow Guyana time to carry out its public consultation). Media reports indicate that the EPA text, with over 1,000 pages, had to be 'legally scrubbed' (i.e. reviewed for legal language and consistency) and translated into all the official EU

course of action.[7] The proposal was strongly critiqued by the CRNM and there was no official response from the heads of government.

Several postponements of the ministerial signing of the EPA, mainly for logistical reasons,[8] allowed the protest movement to gather wider support. In June 2008 a regional network of civil society organizations launched a campaign for EPA renegotiation around four objectives.[9] This appeal was supported by the Caribbean Congress of Labour, a regional network of labour organizations. By August, parliamentary opposition parties in Jamaica, Trinidad and Tobago, Antigua and Barbuda, St Lucia and Dominica had come out against the agreement in its existing form and some governments were reported to be privately unhappy with the agreement. At Caricom's July 2008 summit the split among the leaders continued and Guyana asked for additional time in order to conduct a public EPA consultation. The consultation was held in August and the Guyanese private sector, civil society and the parliamentary opposition gave support to the government's proposal for EPA renegotiation. However, this was strongly opposed by EU negotiators. More importantly, Guyana did not receive the support of other Caricom governments. It was, therefore, politically isolated while facing the EU threat to impose tariffs on the exports of its all-important sugar industry on the European market.

In the end Guyana reluctantly agreed to sign the negotiated EPA (October 2008), but with one important proviso. A joint declaration was adopted which provides for a mandatory review of the agreement within the first five years and thereafter at five-yearly intervals. The effect of this is to open the possibility of an assessment of the developmental and socioeconomic impact of the EPA and of a comprehensive renegotiation by 2013. It was therefore the main achievement of Guyana's stand and of the EPA protest movement. But use of the mandatory review in this way is only a possibility: everything depends on how far governments, civil society and the private sector are prepared to take advantage of it. The issues, the intra-Caricom differences and the external pressures will continue to arise in the future.

Lessons

languages. Caricom governments were also said to be formally reviewing the document and submitting it for formal cabinet approval and parliamentary debate.

The EPA protests registered some successes. They helped to move the EPA into the domain of public debate and to expose it to wider scrutiny by professionals, stakeholders and the media. Civil society organizations became involved, major cracks in elite consensus were exposed, one government both helped to catalyse the protests and aligned itself with it, and the mandatory review undertaking opens opportunities to renegotiate the agreement in the future. Yet they failed to achieve the objective of renegotiation. What lessons can be learnt?

9 Caribbean Policy
Development Centre,
'Renegotiate the EPA
petition', online at
www.normangirvan.
info/renegotiate-the-
epa-petition-cpdc/.
The four points were
(1) limit the EPA to
what is required to
make it WTO-
compatible; (2) make
legally binding
provisions for EC
financial and
technical assistance;
(3) insert legally
binding criteria to
measure
socioeconomic
impacts; and (4)
include a mandatory
review with the
possibility of
renegotiation within
three years of
signature.

First, ACP and Caricom governments handled the negotiations badly. They were 'comprehensively outmanoeuvred' by the European Commission trade directorate led by Trade Commissioner Peter Mandelson (Jessop 2007). Even given that the ACP was forced by the EU to negotiate in six different groups, tactical blunders were subsequently made and the ACP failed to maintain a united front on key issues and strategies. These include:

1   The means of operationalizing the manner in which the EPAs would support development.
2   Inclusion of binding commitments for additional development assistance.
3   Inclusion of measures to address non-tariff barriers in EU markets.
4   Exclusion from EPAs of 'WTO-plus' rules restricting ACP governments' 'policy space'.
5   EU provision of acceptable non-EPA alternatives for accessing the EU market.
6   ACP presentation of coherent regional development plans and strategies as the basis for negotiations.
7   ACP building of political alliances in EU member states, the European parliament and civil society organizations.

Second, the failure of Caricom governments to educate the regional public about the EPA deprived them of the option of mobilizing political support around demands for an improvement in the terms of the agreement. This weakened their negotiating position with the EU and increased their political vulnerability to pressures from exporters who stood to lose from the threatened imposition of EU tariffs. Third, Cariforum's (including Caricom's) enthusiasm in negotiating a 'Full' EPA broke ranks with the rest of the ACP and with the developing country bloc in the WTO, depriving Caricom of the option of seeking international political alliances to support renegotiation of the agreement. In return for this concession, Caricom secured promises of benefits which will be difficult to enforce and on which the Europeans are free to renege, as had happened in the past (MacDonald 2008; Thomas 2008a).

Fourth, given all of the above, the EPA protests were too late, too technical and too lacking in political support to persuade the governments to reopen negotiations on the substance of the agreement. Their format was largely one of lobbying and 'intra-elite communication', employing a technical discourse in the form of memoranda to governments, media commentaries and blog postings. Technical arguments by themselves were insufficient to sway the governments. The issues were too complex to be easily understood and the CRNM, which had an institutional interest in defending the agreement, insisted that its technical knowledge was more authoritative that that of the critics. With such uncertainty, the governments were not prepared to take the political risks of economic disruption represented by the EU threats. To have persuaded the governments to change course, the protests would have had to command strong political support such as massive street protests, defections from the ruling party in parliament, vocal opposition from the business community, or pressure from another powerful external trading partner. The protests from parliamentary opposition parties, however, were relatively muted. Private sector organizations either went quiet or supported the EPA because of fears over loss of export markets and, in the case of service industries, belief that the EPA opens up new export opportunities. The EPA renegotiation campaign of regional civil society and regional labour unions did not attract the level of mass support capable of putting real pressure on the governments: the online petition, which aimed to secure 5,000 signatures, garnered less than 500.

This may be contrasted with the Haitian experience. A similar petition in Haiti secured over 7,500 signatures (Haiti Support Group 2007). The Haitian parliament was publicly lobbied by the 'Stop EPA' campaign and so far the Haitian government has resisted signing the EPA[10]. Two factors that differentiate Haiti is the importance that civil society organizations play in politics and Haiti's international status as a least developed country (LDC). Over the past twenty years Haitian civil society organizations have developed a significant popular base, a capacity for popular education and mobilization, and a sophisticated understanding and critique of neoliberal policies. This was made necessary by the struggles over the election of the first Aristide presidency in 1991, the subsequent coup d'état and repression of the popular movement in 1991–4, the ensuing embrace of neoliberal policies and their continuation during the resumed Aristide presidency of 1994–6, the Preval administration of 1996–2001 and the second Aristide presidency of 2001–4, and related struggles for democratization, debt cancellation and alternative development strategies.

The Stop EPA campaign of Haitian civil society organizations was a logical outgrowth of years of popular agitation against neoliberal policies. It published a document that translated the EPA's implications for ordinary people into popularly accessible language. Moreover, as an LDC, Haiti is entitled to continue to have duty free access to the European market under the EU's 'Everything But Arms' initiative for all LDCs, with or without an EPA. This robbed European negotiators of the ability to threaten Haiti with disruption of its export industries if it refused to sign the EPA. Development aid and debt relief for Haiti are also handled by a group of organizations and countries that is specially constituted for this purpose. They are the subject of separate negotiations between Haiti and its donors, so that Haiti is not reliant on promises of EPA-related assistance from the EU. In short, in Haiti,

10 Haiti's government eventually signed the EPA in November 2009; on terms undisclosed at the time of writing.

the 'pressure from within' against the EPA was greater, and the 'pressure from without' for the agreement was smaller than in the rest of Caricom.

Consider also the situation across a broad swathe of Latin America, where social movements opposed to neoliberal globalization have developed a popular base strong enough to influence government policies, and even change governments. In the last thirty years the two regions have had widely different political trajectories. In Latin America, civil society organizations flourished after the fall of military regimes in the 1980s, but this was also the era of draconian neoliberal policies sponsored by the international financial institutions and codified in the Washington Consensus. By the end of the 1990s Latin America had a 'lived experience' of two decades of neoliberalism with limited improvement in the lot of the majority of the people. Disenchantment with these policies grew, and social movements were radicalized.

In the anglophone Caribbean the progressive movement suffered a number of setbacks in the 1980s: the defeat of Michael Manley's 'democratic socialist' experiment in Jamaica in 1980, the assassination of Walter Rodney in Guyana in the same year, the tragic collapse of the Grenadian Revolution followed by the US invasion of the island in 1983, and the ideological ascendancy of neoliberalism. The decade ended with the collapse of the Soviet Union and of the socialist regimes in Eastern Europe (Abdulah 2008). Caribbean Left organizations and parties, for the most part, disappeared, while emerging NGOs focused on feminist activism, environmental advocacy and grassroots projects. Mainstream political parties embraced pragmatism, which in practice meant policy convergence around the Washington Consensus and acceptance of the basic features of the prevailing model. Trade preferences granted to the region by Europe, the United States and Canada shielded the Caribbean from the full effects of trade liberalization, although the phasing out of EU preferences for its banana exports during the 1990s was a signal lesson in the effects of globalization. Emigration and the return flow of remittances provided a safety valve for those sections of the Caribbean population hardest hit by structural adjustment programmes. Hence, criticisms of the EPA were not grounded in lived experience, while the threat of dislocation resulting from not signing the agreement was immediate and easily understood.

Fifth, the amorphous character of governance in Cariforum and Caricom compounded the challenges for citizen advocacy. Cariforum is not a regional intergovernmental organization with a juridical personality and a transparent system of decision-making with which non-state actors can formally engage. Citizen interventions can only take place through national polities and through Caricom organs. But Caricom governance institutions lack formal provision for citizen involvement, such as a parliament or similar forum. There is the added complication of overlapping structures of decision-making in Caricom. The CRNM reported to the Caricom Prime Ministerial Subcommittee on External Economic Negotiations, the Caricom Council for Trade and Economic Development (COTED), and the Caricom Conference of Heads of Government. The Dominican Republic is also a member of the CRNM, and the processes by which the negotiating positions of the Dominican Republic and of Caricom were harmonized within Cariforum were not transparent. The CRNM is generally perceived to have operated with a significant degree of autonomy in the negotiations process, which promoted a disconnect from the Caricom integration process and facilitated alignment with the European Commission negotiating agenda (Brewster 2008; Thomas 2008b). CRNM dependence on donor funding may have been a contributing factor. Language differences also posed difficulties for cross-Cariforum political collaboration among civil society organizations.

Conclusions: The Technification-Sweetification-Treatyfication Syndrome

In concluding, we propose that the EPA affair was characterized by a 'Technification-Sweetification-Treatyfication' (TST) syndrome, one which may have wider application in theorizing on the political economy of neoliberal trade agreements. *Technification* refers both to the issues that are the subject of negotiations (issue technification) and to the language that is employed to explain the issues to decision-makers, stakeholders and the general public (discourse technification). Issue technification is intrinsic to the substance of these agreements, but discourse technification is not. In principle, any technical issue should be susceptible to explanation to the general population in language that it can understand, for without this the democratic process cannot function effectively. Discourse technification, we would argue, is the result of a political decision to restrict participation in decision-making, since the use of technical language renders the substantive issues inaccessible to non-specialists. Negotiators also have an incentive to retain a monopoly over technical understanding of the agreement, as this maximizes their leverage and provides a means of rebutting critics. Trade expertise then assumes the status of a 'high science' in which a small number of persons wield considerable decision-making power.

Sweetification refers to the highlighting of potential benefits and the downplaying of potential costs of the EPA in presenting it to stakeholders. Provisions are included that promise development assistance and export opportunities which can be used as the material in the public relations exercise of 'selling' the agreement. The provisions, however, are framed in terms that are difficult or impossible to legally enforce. Used in combination, technification and sweetification neutralize opposition, facilitate political acceptance and provide governments with a lexicon of justification for the agreement.

The full implications of the agreement only become apparent in the implementation stage and over an extended period of time. Hence, the crucial role of *treatyfication* – endowing the EPA with the force of international treaty law buttressed by binding arbitration enforced by the threat of trade sanctions in the event of disputes. This is the 'lock-in' effect on government laws and policies: it circumscribes governments' policy space and restricts the scope for the politics of protest. Governments may chafe at the agreement and they may blame their predecessors, but the economic and political costs of reneging on it may be too great to contemplate. Treatyfication therefore subverts democratic governance and national sovereignty. Believers in neoliberalism see this as a virtue, for governments cannot always be relied on to stay the course.

The way to counter the TST syndrome is by a deliberate programme of technical demystification, popular education and political organization. Negotiating texts need to be liberated from technical jargon and translated into language categories that ordinary people can relate to their lived experience.[11] The anti-neoliberal free trade campaigns of Haitian civil society organizations, Latin American social movements and NGOs in other regions have registered many successes in demystifying trade agreements, as did the campaign of the global civil society movement against the Multilateral Agreement on Investment. In the Caribbean, the potential is shown by the progress made by the EPA protest movement in including a variety of stakeholders within a relatively short period of time.

Finally, note may be taken of the 'participation dilemma' that affects civil society in trade negotiations. Mechanisms for CSO involvement in negotiations provide an opportunity to impact outcomes: they are also a device for political co-optation and of legitimization of bad outcomes. In the Cariforum EPA negotiations, civil society consultations took place within a negotiating framework that had been previously established with embedded assumptions on the kind of agreement that would emerge at the end of the process (Thomas 2008c). Hence, objectionable subject areas were included in the negotiating template from the outset, while socioeconomic issues of interest to civil society were not built into the architecture of the agreement. The answer to the dilemma is simultaneous participation at both the technical and political level and both within the negotiations process and in the public domain. Civil society stakeholders will need to master the technical intricacies of negotiations, to translate the implications into socially meaningful categories, and to develop the kind of political weight capable of impacting governmental decision-making. For this, long-term sustained effort will be necessary.

11 Examples of translating EPA issues into relatively simple accessible language are Haiti Support Group (2007), Oxfam (2008), and the documents of Third World Network (www.twnside.org) and www.bilaterals,org.

References

Abdulah, D. (2008) 'Social movements in the Caribbean: solidarity, building of alliances and convergences, struggles and the new threats of criminalization of protests, Fourth Assembly of Caribbean Peoples, Havana, 28 June–5 July, online at www.normangirvan.info/category/epa-text-and-commentaries/norman-girvans-epa-papers/ (accessed 12 May 2009).

ACP-EEC (1975) ACP-EEC convention signed at, Lomé, 28 February, online at www.acpsec.org/en/conventions/lome1.htm (accessed 11 May 2009).

ACP-EEC (2000) The Cotonou Agreement, 23 June 2000, online at www.acpsec.org/en/conventions/cotonou/accord1.htm (accessed 11 May 2009).

Atarah, L. (1999) 'WTO rules used to kill Lomé Convention, NGOs say', TWN, 5 October, online at www.twnside.org.sg/title/lome-cn.htm (accessed 10 May 2009).

Bartels, L. (2007) 'Legal opinion on ACP legal options to maintain market access', Cambridge, 23 November, online at www.normangirvan.info/legal-opinion-on-acp-legal-options-to-maintain-market-access-by-dr-lorand-bartels-trade-lawyer-cambridge-university/ (accessed 10 May 2009).

Bartels, L. (2008) 'Comment on the Cariforum-EU EPA', Brussels, 22 February, online at www.normangirvan.info/legal-aspects-of-the-Cariforum-ec-epa-dr-loren-bartels-february-13-2008/ (accessed 9 May 2009).

Brewster, H. (2008) 'Political and policy lessons from the Cariforum EPA: note prepared for the CARICOM secretariat, Georgetown, 16 January 2008', online at www.normangirvan.info/political-and-policy-lessons-from-the-epa-negotiations-have-lock-brewster/ (accessed 12 May 2009).

Brewster, H., Girvan, N. and Lewis, V. (2008) 'Renegotiate the EPA', COTED, Georgetown, 27 February, online at www.normangirvan.info/renegotiate-epa/ (accessed 13 May 2009).

European Commission (2006a) 'European Union to commit EU 22 billion in aid to Africa, the Caribbean and the Pacific Islands, IP/06/710', Brussels, 1 June, online at www.europa.eu/rapid/pressReleasesAction.do?reference=IP/06/710&format=HTML&aged=0&language=EN&guiLanguage=en (accessed 9 May 2009).

European Commission (2006b) Partnership agreement EC-ACP, signed in Cotonou, 23 June 2000, revised in Luxembourg 25 August 2005. EC DE-132, September 2006, online at www.ec.europa.eu/development/icenter/repository/Cotonou_EN_2006_en.pdf (accessed 9 May 2009).

Haiti Support Group (2007) Declaration of the Haitian coalition, 'Block the EPA' ('Bare APE' in Creole), in the context of Haiti's participation in the negotiation of Partnership Agreements between the European Union and the ACP countries, Port-au-Prince, 17 October, online at www.haitisupport.gn.apc.org/EPA.html (accessed 11 August 2009).

Jessop, D. (2007) 'The view from Europe: EPA EC options', 26 October, online at www.caribbean-council.org/consultancy/publications/TheViewfromEurope.htm (accessed 10 May 2009).

MacDonald, I. (2008) 'A partnership we could not refuse', *Stabroek News*, 13 January, online at www.normangirvan.info/epa-in-the-media/ (accessed 10 May 2009).

Oxfam (2008) 'Partnership or power play?' 21 April, online at www.normangirvan.info/wp-content/uploads/2008/04/oxfam-partnership-or-power-play.pdf (accessed 13 May 2009).

Seattle to Brussels Network (2006) 'The new "Global Europe" strategy of the EU: serving corporations worldwide and at home', 2 December, online at www.bilaterals.org/IMG/pdf/globaleurope_s2balert_nov06.pdf (accessed 25 July 2008).

Stevens, C. (2007) 'Costs to the ACP of exporting to the EU under the GSP',Overseas Development Institute, London, March, online at www.hubrural.org/pdf/odi_acp_gsp_report.pdf (accessed 9 May 2009).

Thomas, C. (2008a) 'Guyana and the wider world', *Starbroek News*, 20 January, online at www.stabroeknews.com/2008/features/sunday/01/20/guyana-and-the-wider-world-8/ > (accessed 10 May 2009).

Thomas, C. (2008b) 'Guyana and the wider world', *Starbroek News*, 24 February, online at www.stabroeknews.com/2008/features/sunday/02/24/guyana-and-the-wider-world-13/ (accessed 12 May 2009).

Thomas, C. (2008c) 'CARICOM perspectives on the Cariforum-EC Economic Partnership Agreement (EPA)', Georgetown, May, online at www.normangirvan.info/wp-content/uploads/2008/05/clive-thomas-Caricom-perspective-on-the-cf-ec-epa-may-2008.pdf (accessed 12 May 2009).

SHIFTING THE GROUND BENEATH US
Social Reproduction, Grassroots Women's Organizing and the 2005 Floods in Guyana

D. Alissa Trotz
University of Toronto, Canada

Nearly three decades after the implementation of structural adjustment programmes, there are rapidly growing social and economic inequalities in the Caribbean, a situation further aggravated in Guyana by a divided and highly racialized political landscape. This essay looks at how Red Thread, a Guyanese women's organization, draws on women's caring work to ground various interventions that contest the status quo and span traditional racialized and spatialized divisions in the country. Beginning with an account of feminist rearticulations of social reproduction as critical feminist praxis, the essay grounds this conceptual frame in a discussion of the January 2005 floods that devastated Guyana's coastal communities and affected some 40 per cent of the population. It focuses specifically on how Red Thread organized with grassroots women to challenge official narratives of the floods, to make women's work visible and to come up with a list of demands that brought women together across several communities. It concludes with a discussion of the effects of the mobilization, and how it demonstrates a commitment to engaging women as a diverse collectivity through working out rather than assuming a politics of connection and affiliation.

> It is only direct action on the part of the people, your own perception of what is possible, that can produce fundamental change. (Walter Rodney, 1982)

Introduction

The difficulties facing the Caribbean today include over two decades of unmitigated structural adjustment programmes (SAPs), a bankrupt neocolonial state structure, a disaffected population increasingly cynical of party politics, the atomization of social relations, alarming levels of violence and unprecedented levels of out-migration. In Guyana, twenty four years of rigged polls finally gave way to democratic elections in 1992, monopolized by African and Indian Guyanese (the country's demographic majority) voting for one or the other of the two main political parties. This situation has contributed to mistrust, violence, racialized insecurities and instability, while partly providing an easy alibi for the government (securely in power for the last seventeen years) to evade difficult questions about corruption, the continuation of authoritarian practices, and the devastating effects of neoliberal policies. Without denying the very real challenges these present for radical alternatives, this essay deliberately looks for something else, an epistemological shift that is made possible by rearticulating social reproduction as critical feminist praxis in Guyana.

Hierarchical relations underpin the organization of social reproduction, understood here as the physical and emotional (caring) labour involved in the everyday and generational maintenance of life itself. Early efforts to extend Marxist notions of production fruitfully theorized the domestic domain as a key site of social reproduction, foregrounding unwaged work (which principally falls on women) as both indispensable subsidy to capitalism and invisible from its calculations of value (Dalla Costa and James 1972). More recent interventions highlight how the 'messiness' of 'life's work' makes it impossible to sustain abstract separations between production and reproduction, or to see these as occurring in distinct, non-overlapping spaces (Mitchell, Marston and Katz 2003). The crisis of social reproduction under neoliberalism – the downsizing of the state, further devolution of responsibilities to the household and individual level – has also sparked interest in comparative and transnational research that attends to the ways in which this relationship plays out across a variety of scales, and identifies potentially new political responses and actors (Bakker and Gill 2003; Mitchell, Marston and Katz, 2003).

In an important essay that attempts to address this issue, Cindi Katz (2001) reformulates topography – the layered description and delineation of a landscape – as a critical and interested research method that can follow and challenge the uneven effects of globalization by excavating the spatialized flows and relations that inflect practices of social reproduction in distinct, localized ways. This becomes the basis for generating counter-topographies, in which a particular constellation of practices is scrupulously 'connected to other specific topographies affected by global processes in analogous ways', and where the link is forged not through generalizations but through the elaboration of 'precise analytic relationships' or 'contour lines' (Katz 2001: 1229). This approach adds a critical dimension to feminist situated knowledges, for it recognizes the importance of explicating location as the generative ground for knowing, while simultaneously insisting on situatedness (the ground for/under identity) as precisely that which requires interrogation. For Katz, the insights that derive from the 'critical triangulation of local topographies [can] provide ... the impulse for insurgent change' (1232), challenging us to track *how* such a reorientation might engender meaningful shifts – and by *whom* – that decentre the neoliberal model and offer alternative maps of connection. What are the processes through which a feminist counter-topography might come to life as a radically different oppositional politics?

Cecilia Green (2001) offers a promising point of departure with which we might begin to answer this question, in her historical-materialist and popular-feminist reconfiguration of Caribbean dependency theory. Key to her discussion is an incisive critique of the circumscription of the economic in some of these earlier frameworks to privilege the 'marketplace', the 'law' and the 'government', consigning the informal and domestic economy and those located within it, the working (waged and unwaged) poor, to marginality or invisibility. Green urges us to attend 'not only [to] the commanding heights of the economy and its hegemonic force but also the nooks, crannies and living networks of the popular and domestic economy and its creative potential' (Green 2001: 68). It is a potential that was visible in the 1970s and 1980s, in the mobilization of women to protest against the early implementation of SAP's in Trinidad and Tobago and exploitative working conditions in free trade zones in Jamaica (Reddock 1998), as well as in the tentative efforts of Jamaican women in urban garrison communities to create violence-free zones in their neighbourhoods (Harrison 1997). A renewed Caribbean radicalism built upon a sturdy 'politics of empowerment' starts with those who inhabit these spaces, and requires looking with different eyes to construct a more inclusive and dynamic angle of vision that can potentially rescript dominant narratives while itself being transformed in the process (Green 2001: 69; see also Haraway 1997).

This essay takes up this challenge through an examination of how Red Thread, a women's organization in Guyana, responded to floods that devastated the country's coast in 2005. Katz's emphasis on the instability of place resonates with the disappearance of the ground that Guyanese stood on during the heavy rains, offering a template to 'link different places analytically and thereby enhance struggles in the name of common interests' (Katz 2001: 1230). In what follows, I shall attempt to trace how the epistemological shift advocated by Green materialized, through a self-conscious emphasis on social reproduction as the contour line for bringing grassroots women together across different communities.[1]

Formed in 1986 by a small group of middle-class women who were then members of the multi-racial Working People's Alliance (WPA), from its inception Red Thread defined itself as an autonomous organization located firmly outside of party structures. This non-negotiable commitment was a local response to the racialized – African-Guyanese and Indian-Guyanese – constituencies that formed the membership and compromised the independence of the women's arms of the two main political parties, and was put into a regional context for several members by the collapse of the women's arm of the People's Revolutionary Government of Grenada in 1983 (Andaiye 2000; Nettles 2007).

Guyana has long had a progressive legal framework on matters relating to gender equality, the combined result of the strong involvement of women in anticolonial and nationalist politics, and the fact that all of the major political parties come out of a Left tradition that has afforded greater – albeit still limited – space to engage these issues. Beginning in the 1970s, and under the rule of the People's National Congress (PNC), cooperative socialist policies emphasizing self-sufficiency (under the highly gendered slogan 'Feed, Clothe and House the Nation') resulted in extensive nationalization and a vastly expanded bureaucracy, increasing formal sector employment opportunities for women, and for African-Guyanese women in particular. Although the role of the state was enhanced as public provider of social goods such as free education and healthcare, the gendered distribution of unwaged work in the home was never substantially addressed as related to the economy or as a key issue for a socialist agenda (Peake 1993). As the country teetered on the brink of political and economic collapse from the late 1970s, it was these invisible sectors that increasingly assumed responsibility for community sustenance, via the growing privatization of social reproduction and the intensification of women's involvement in the informal and unwaged sectors. The introduction of the Economic Recovery Programme in 1986 (the local iteration of structural adjustment, dubbed Empty Rice Pot by Guyanese) exacerbated and in some ways institutionalized (through official policies of state disinvestment) these arrangements.

In a recent essay, Red Thread founder-member Andaiye reflected on the independent contributions of grassroots women across race to the food rebellions of the early 1980s at the height of the anti-dictatorial struggle (involvement in street protests, participation in the parallel economy as traders smuggling contraband food items into the country), which challenged shortages, rations and bans on several items essential to the Guyanese diet.

1 The material on which this analysis is based draws upon video and unpublished reports produced by Red Thread, as well as ongoing conversations with Red Thread members over the past four years. I observed the second national Red Thread/GWAR meeting, as well as several small GWAR/Red Thread discussions, and was a participant-observer at several of the jointly staged demonstrations. With Maya Trotz I helped design and update a flood-related website in 2005 that also served to raise funds for the Alecia Foundation which Red Thread initially partnered with (www.jouvay.com/guyana). Thanks to organizers and participants in the Remembering a Future Caribbean conference, and to Ashwini Tambe, for helpful comments.

She suggested that no one in the WPA, including those who comprised the Women's Section of the party, fully grasped 'that what we were seeing was a sector of the working people in motion', concluding in relation to Red Thread that 'it took fifteen years for two of us who, in 1983 were WPA women, to draw the lessons and to begin to attempt – slowly and gradually (given a far less favourable environment) – a way of organizing based on the recognition of grassroots housewives as a sector of the working class and their unwaged labour as the foundation of the whole economy' (Andaiye 2008; see also Dalla Costa and James 1972).

Today, two of Red Thread's nine core full-time members are from the group of founders; the remaining seven, as well as the women who constitute the organization's expanding local network, comprise grassroots women from urban, rural and hinterland communities. One of Red Thread's original goals was to build solidarity among women across divides. In the last decade, and through individual associations with the global Wages for Housework Campaign and then Red Thread's decision to officially join the anti-imperialist anti-racist Global Women's Strike network as a national coordinator when it formed in 2000, this objective has been focalized through an explicit emphasis on beginning with and politicizing the caring work of grassroots women. Counting women's work now serves as the framework for all of Red Thread's efforts to connect across local and transnational spaces. The question of *who* does the counting is equally critical, as exemplified by Red Thread's unprecedented and extensive time-use survey, conducted by and with grassroots women across Guyana. The survey was intended not only to make work visible and matter in a different way, but to use the knowledge generated to organize in response to identified needs. This shift is crucial to understanding Red Thread's response to the floods of January 2005.

From Relief to Organizing: The 2005 Floods

In his seminal *History of the Guyanese Working People* (1981), Walter Rodney lays bare the human endeavour that transformed swamplands into habitable ground through an intricate system of empoldering. For the nearly ninety per cent of the population that makes their home on the narrow coastal strip that lies several feet below sea level, 'mud and flood are essential components of the historical record of Guyanese life' (Westmaas 2005). In January 2005 this precarious territorialization was devastatingly under-scored when a heavier than usual rainy season – indicative of ominously shifting weather patterns – resulted in the most devastating floods in Guyana's history, directly affecting close to forty per cent of the population. Entire communities lived under stagnant and contaminated water (more than four feet deep in some places), accessible by boat or the vessels – upturned fridges, boards lashed to oil drums – improvised by residents. The shelters that the government opened offered temporary relief to less than 6,000 persons, leading many to decamp to the coastal main road in search of dry land, food and potable water. Households suffered extensive losses that included furniture and personal effects, vegetable gardens, farmlands, poultry, livestock and outdoor equipment. Of the thirty four deaths, seven were due to drowning; the rest were the result of flood-related illnesses, with hundreds admitted to hospital.

If flooding is not new, the historic damage wrought by the January 2005 rains was amplified by and symptomatic of the hollowing out of the Guyanese state following over two decades of IMF-imposed structural adjustment policies:

> lack of will on the part of the authorities; unresponsiveness of governments to warnings and people's plight; political interference and corruption at state and local governance [levels] ... political and social collapse of infrastructure, the fleeing of skills, the hapless City Council, and the slide in civic-mindedness that allowed businesses and householders to drop garbage in the drains and trenches. (Westmaas 2005).

A few days after the floods, Red Thread (some of whose members lived in heavily flooded communities) participated in a series of meetings that led to the establishment of the Guyana Citizens' Initiative (GCI), a loose grouping of activists, community leaders and professionals that sought to develop a broad-based and non-partisan flood and disaster preparedness response (www.gci.org.gy; accessed 15 March 2009). Together with the GCI and the Alicea Foundation (a charitable organization with a focus on women's education, health and 'the relief of poverty, disease and sickness'), Red Thread participated in the delivery of flood relief to severely affected coastal communities, targeting 'elderly people, pregnant and breast-feeding mothers, people with disabilities and women with young children', all categories of persons who they had come to recognize were being trapped in their homes by the floodwaters. At the time, this was an initial response to the fact that none of the relief efforts or official pronouncements was specifically recognizing the gendered distribution of vulnerability or the ways in which women were assuming particular responsibilities in relation to their households. In addition to packaging and distributing hampers, Red Thread helped organize medical clinics, with a team of doctors and nurses treating over 1,000 persons at several shelters set up over two days.

Notwithstanding the importance of distributing aid, such efforts, taken in isolation, ran the risk of privileging charity as the mode of engaging the poor, deflecting attention away from the need to address the longer-term structural issues that mediated the impact of the floods. Red Thread was at any rate always interested in moving from providing relief to organizing with communities (or at least to linking these two), a position that was reinforced as people travelled to their offices seeking material support. Shifting the terms of their engagement with those affected by the floods emerged as members began holding meetings with women in over two dozen coastal communities. In contrast to the dominant tendency in official efforts in which affected persons might best be described as supplicants or recipients of technical know-how (one symbol of this distance was the television images and descriptions given of relief personnel sitting safely in boats throwing packages at residents wading through chest-high and often stagnant waters to catch them), these sessions reworked the definition of knowledge producers. They were less about information dissemination (even when framed in this way, information was offered to respond to the immediate realities of grassroots women's lives *as articulated by them*, and related to such topics as basic water treatment procedures for bathing, cooking and drinking, garbage disposal, disinfecting and cleaning houses and yards), than about the kinds of gendered knowledge that emerged through the collective process of discussing the floods. One telling example relates to the women's determination to recoup their losses, which entailed making visible the kinds of responsibilities – and the material needs associated with them – that they defined as critical to sustaining their families. It soon became clear that public discussions were framing costs primarily through a definition of losses tied exclusively to income-generating activities, an emphasis that highlighted the absence of grassroots women from broader debates about compensation. Rather than fitting them into existing databases designed to tabulate losses as a basis for making claims, the concept of livelihoods had to be fundamentally rethought to address the women's own accounting of the multi-dimensionality of their lives:

> The women's definition of livelihood is everything that goes into the care of their families, especially their children … we had to redo [the claim form] including their household items, what they used to produce, especially food for household use, and what they used to produce goods for sale or the goods themselves. They did not accept that their small kitchen garden or the livestock or poultry which they used to feed the household should be treated differently from say, the farm of a cash crop farmer. (Red Thread 2006).

If getting grassroots women to meet inside of their villages was the first step to formulating a public intervention, making links beyond one's immediate environment was key to crafting a collective platform. Community meetings distilled the various issues into a list of specific demands that were further refined and endorsed at a public session. The information sheet that was distributed around the country to publicize the meeting represented a strategic intervention into the public sphere. Situating the speakout within the Global Women's Strike framework (for which Red Thread serves as the Guyana coordinator), the handbill insisted that unwaged caring work produces value, and singled out Venezuela as the one example of grassroots women's mobilization contributing to this principle being incorporated into the Bolivarian Constitution as Article 88. Positioning these issues as a specific instance of global forces and resistant responses offered a larger canvas to map potential transnational connections, while serving as reminder that within the context of even the most resolutely local, there were relationships across place that could also be made. Moreover, naming the Venezuelan Constitution drew attention to shifts taking place in Guyana's own backyard, providing a most proximate example of what grassroots women could dare to imagine together.

We might read this intervention as restoring a transnational dimension to a reinvigorated notion of the political in Guyana, drawing on a legacy of international solidarity – present during the anticolonial coalition that resulted in the 1953 victory at the polls and also later, during the 1970s – that shaped the experiences of an older generation of Guyanese. This broader dimension is largely absent today, except as a consciousness mobilized in relation to individual and familial migratory strategies. It also interrupts state-focused discourses in which Venezuela is cast as regional pariah by the United States, ambivalently positioned in contemporary representations of its relationship to the Caribbean,[2] or portrayed as an ever present threat to Guyana's border security. This dominant geopolitical framing was challenged by offering a people-centred route to engaging Guyana's hemispheric neighbour, and builds on Red Thread's ongoing work with the Global Women's Strike and their earlier visit, in January 2006, to the World Social Forum in Venezuela, where they met with women from the Network.[3]

Returning to the local scale, the handbill foregrounded how survival was in fact enabled by the work of 'the grassroots women of every race who braved waist-deep and even chest-deep flood waters … to invent ways to feed, clothe, shelter, teach, nurse, worry about and provide safety and a sense of security for their children first of all' (Speakout Handout). Asking why these experiences had been ignored threw into stark relief how existing flood narratives were underpinned by a distorted and narrow set of priorities, framed in discourses that were highly technocratic and that positioned those most affected as dependents. Inviting the public to hear from grassroots women underlined how society is indebted to social reproduction, creating the space for a vocabulary of entitlements.

'Grassroots Women Speak Out: Counting Our Work for Guyana's Survival from the Flood', was held in Georgetown on 13 March 2005.

2 President Hugo Chávez's overtures to the Caribbean, most notably in relation to the proposed Petrocaribe project, have been described alternately as a genuine attempt to forge a hemispheric alliance that bypasses US hegemony, and as Venezuela trying to flex its muscles in the Caribbean.
3 For a brief report of this visit, see www.global womenstrike.net/ Guyana/ GuyanaVenezuela Report.htm#Guyana VenezuelaReport (accessed 20 May 2009).

Representatives from the media, parliament, trade unions, government units, local NGOs and international donor agencies were invited, but in a reversal of the usual roles of expert and passive audience, the meeting was structured around testimonies from the more than two hundred women gathered. Small groups caucused and then convened to put together a final statement that foregrounded caring work, distinguished between short-, medium- and long-term objectives, encompassed household, community, national and international spaces and addressed state as well as non-state actors:

- It addressed immediate flood issues (decrying the politicization and uneven distribution of relief; calling for cleanup action and soil and water testing; proposing that persons from communities most affected should be the first to be offered any employment generated by the cleaning activities).
- It went beyond limited notions of flood-related compensation by highlighting how gender, race, class and disability mediated the distribution of vulnerability (calling for a cancellation of household debt; stressing the need to address historic levels of poverty that existed *prior* to the floods and differentiated people's ability to escape or mitigate the damage).
- It raised the issue of accountability (demanding an audit of how monies received for relief efforts – across all sectors – were spent; calling for an independent inquiry and the meaningful inclusion of communities in disaster preparedness discussions).
- It recognized how the crisis pertained to Guyana's structural vulnerability in the international system (calling for the cancellation of Guyana's national debt).

Assessing the Speakout: Whose Yardstick?

How does one begin to assess the effects of this campaign? At a meeting on 9 March 2005, Bibi Shadick from the Ministry of Labour, Human Services and Social Security, noted, in a statement welcomed by Red Thread, that 'it is the women of Guyana who defended their children from disease and death during the flood'. The question is, what did this discursive recognition translate into with respect to the specific demands of the speakout? Livestock owners received veterinary assistance from the Ministry of Agriculture, the United Nations Development Programme provided chickens, seeds, sewing machines and freezers for women in some communities, and schools were comprehensively cleaned by the Ministry of Education. Shortly after the speakout, the government also decided to offer G$10,000 to affected households, a sum that was not only inadequate in the face of the losses sustained, but that did not recognize the differentiated vulnerabilities that the women's focus on caring work had highlighted.

There has also been little consultation between the government and communities on infrastructural repair and maintenance, and virtually nothing in the way of a consistent national campaign to engage the public as active participants. Heavy rainfall in December of 2008 once again resulted in floods, with the damage this time spreading to encompass a wider area than in 2005. The water did not remain on the land for nearly as long, but raised serious questions about the extensive monies supposedly spent on repair and construction (there has been little accountability and practically no information forthcoming on such things as how the tenders were awarded; additionally, only the Alecia Foundation and the Red Cross provided any information on the receipt and spending of relief monies in 2005), while pointing to serious and persistent weaknesses in the proper maintenance of drainage systems, solid waste management and disaster preparedness (Roopnaraine 2009).

While the results might be described as sobering when evaluated in this way, Red Thread's own assessment, coming one year after the 2005 floods, offered a different kind of environmental audit: 'In spite of the fact that we didn't gain enough by organizing, women organizing within and across communities in their own interests and with their own perspective is crucially important. We didn't win enough but we think we would have gained far less if we had not' (Red Thread 2006).

This is not a matter of being realistic or having modest goals, but about recognizing the fits and starts that accompany collective political engagement, particularly when the intervention offers something radically different from usual modes of participation. As Cecilia Green notes:

A key tool in the pursuit of empowerment is understanding how ordinary people – women and men – have invented themselves, their lives and their livelihoods, and how they both suffer and evade victimization on an everyday level ... I am not suggesting that with such understanding something magical will occur; politics (and a different kind of politics, in different arenas) has to be built, devised, strategized, organized according to its own logic, not just inferred. (Green 2001: 68–9)

It is important to put the 'results' into perspective by remembering that the speakout was the culmination of less than six weeks of mobilizing with grassroots women. The successes that materialized therefore served as a visible marker of what could be achieved, while grassroots women demonstrated to themselves and others their viability as agentive political actors, through their creation of a space beyond the isolation of individual households and contiguous communities. The list of demands they generated might best be read as future-oriented, a strategic manifesto that signalled an intention to continue organizing beyond this immediate crisis.

The emphasis on social reproduction also proved to be a very effective way for grassroots women to generate their own analyses. It prompted a reconsideration of income-based understandings of livelihoods, made visible the multiplier effects of the damage by pointing out how income-generating activities relied heavily on a multiplicity of transactions among community members, and highlighted the kinds of challenges women faced (from caring for children to contracting urinary and other infections as a result of wading through filthy water). Specific issues also emerged, such as the invisibility of women with disabilities, the hardship faced by single-parent households, and the sense that the proportion of single mothers was far higher (especially among Indo-Guyanese women) than official estimates (Red Thread 2006).

Finally, this was arguably the first time since the anti-dictatorial struggles of the 1970s and 1980s that grassroots women entered the national political imagination in this way. For Red Thread, perhaps the most important outcome was that 'the organizing got Indo-Guyanese women from different parts of the East Coast and Afro-Guyanese women especially from Buxton in the same room to interact in a meaningful way and to organize together in their own interest'. The reference to Buxton is important; once heralded as one of the earliest free villages bought and settled by Africans in the post-emancipation period, representing a proud tradition of independence and resistance, Buxton today is more frequently stereotyped as the launching pad for criminal activity and violence against Indian-Guyanese communities (Trotz 2004).[4] It is important to historicize these contemporary fault lines in order to consider the external destabilization and tragic collapse of a multi-racial, anticolonial movement in the 1950s, which would explode into the racial disturbances of the 1960s and occasion massive internal displacement. Political independence, coming in 1966 on the heels of the unrest and the reconfiguration of the coast into far more racially homogeneous villages, ushered in a period of divisive electoral politics that has been consolidated rather than dissolved with the return to electoral democracy in 1992. Such racialized political loyalties have severely impeded possibilities for non-partisan 'citizen politics' (Gray 2007). Against this backdrop, the speakout offered a potential third space beyond the isolation of neighbouring villages increasingly defined in antagonistic relationships of difference. Its counter-topographical praxis (Katz 2001) entailed an anti-racist spatial politics that refused sedimented impulses by drawing other lines of connection across communities that revealed hierarchies within them: 'We are from all the races in Guyana and from all political parties, some of us from no political party; the flood did not discriminate among us. This is not about party politics but about women and survival politics. Anyone who tries to break us up is against women and our families surviving' (Red Thread n.d.: 4).

4 One cannot underestimate the difficulties of this bridging work, in the face of deeply entrenched mistrust and interruptions of violence like the horrific slaughter in January 2008 of eleven women, men and children in Lusignan (a village described today as Indian Guyanese), followed by the massacre of twelve men in the riverain community of Bartica less than three weeks later. Residents of Buxton have also been resentful and highly critical of the ways in which they have been stereotyped, of an intrusive military and police presence, and of the unlawful arrest and detention of – primarily – young African-Guyanese men.

Although indigenous communities were not as directly affected by the 2005 floods, Amerindian women were also invited to attend the speakout in a deliberate attempt to confront the coastal-hinterland division and generate new solidaristic spaces.

Out of the flood organizing, a network, Guyanese Women Across Race (GWAR), was established with grassroots women from urban, rural and indigenous communities. GWAR, along with Red Thread members, have since held two national meetings (in the second meeting, held in December 2008, participants came from twenty communities on the coast and hinterland). They have initiated surveys to track changes in the cost of living and the effects of value-added tax, compiled report cards to evaluate the platforms of political parties beyond the election campaign cycle, and participated in various demonstrations against violence, child abuse and the cost of living. In the most recent floods the GCI facilitated Red Thread's meetings with women from several newly affected villages (GCI 2008). Red Thread has also participated in Global Strike international gatherings in Venezuela and Mexico City; at the most recent meetings in London, they were joined by a GWAR member from an indigenous community.

Consolidating the network through these related interventions has not been a straightforward affair. There is no easy assumption here of 'grassroots women' as a homogenized, romanticized constituency, but recognizing difference in the Guyanese context is a tricky proposition that always runs the risk of reproducing lines that are strictly drawn. Red Thread demonstrates that while we begin from where (and who) we are, the process of engagement also has the potential to shift the ground from under us, requiring us to rethink our relationships to each other and revealing territory and identity to be contingent and – therefore – open to change: 'One critical experience of women organizing to restore their livelihoods is that since we are organizing across race, while the women continue to see themselves as discriminated against on the grounds of race and continue to express all kinds of racial insecurities and hostilities, they have also begun to see the similarities in their livelihoods as women who are poor' (Red Thread 2006). Andaiye (2008) puts it best: 'we are not interested in a politics of identity, but a politics of transformation, starting with women.'

Without trivializing their deadly material effects, we might see the floods as a metaphor – in the sense of lessons learned – for the ground shifting under us, for the instability and indeterminacy of politics. Where outcomes are concerned, there really are no guarantees. The process – of meeting, sharing, listening, counting, valuing, demanding – that begins with the caring work of grassroots women, and that has led to the emergence and growth of the network, is indicative of a commitment to seeing women as a diverse collectivity that does not stand still, and to working out, rather than assuming, the politics of connection and affiliation at multiple levels. In contemporary Guyana, rearticulating social reproduction as critical anti-racist feminist praxis promises an alternative and more inclusive vision than the one that currently shapes and limits the horizon of possibility.

References

Andaiye (2000) 'The Red Thread story', in S. Francis-Brown (ed.) *Spitting in the Wind: Lessons in Empowerment from the Caribbean*, Kingston, Jamaica: Ian Randle Publishers, pp. 51–98.

Andaiye (2008) 'Making grassroots women across race visible in the Guyanese resistance of the seventies and early eighties for which Walter Rodney was a point of reference.' Presented at the Walter Rodney Conference, Centre for Caribbean Thought, University of the West Indies, Mona, Jamaica, 16–18 October.

Bakker, I. and Gill, S. (2003) *Power, Production and Social Reproduction: Human In/security in the Global Political Economy*, Basingstoke: Palgrave Macmillan.

Dalla Costa, M. and James, S. (1972) *The Power of Women and the Subversion of Community*, London: Falling Wall Press.

Gray, O. (2007) 'Civic politics in Jamaica: new populism or political breakthrough?' in B. Meeks (ed.) *Culture, Politics, Race and Diaspora: The Thought of Stuart Hall*, Kingston, Jamaica: University of the West Indies Press, pp. 185–96.

Green, C. (2001) 'Caribbean dependency theory of the 1970s: a historical-materialist-feminist revision', in B. Meeks and F. Lindahl (eds) *New Caribbean Thought: A Reader*, Kingston, Jamaica: University of the West Indies Press, pp. 40–72.

Guyana Citizens' Initiative (2008) December/January flood reports and media releases.

Haraway, D. (1997) 'The persistence of vision', in K. Conboy, N. Medina and S. Stanbury (eds) *Writing on the Body*, 7th edn, New York: Columbia University Press, pp. 283–95.

Harrison, F. V. (1997) 'The gendered politics and violence of structural adjustment', in L. Lamphere, H. Ragoné and P. Zavella (eds) *Situated Lives: Gender and Culture in Everyday Life*, New York: Routledge, pp. 451–68.

Katz, C. (2001) 'On the grounds of globalization: a topography for feminist political engagement', *Signs* 26(4): 1213–34.

Mitchell, K., Marston, S. A. and Katz, C. (2003) 'Introduction: life's work: an introduction, review and critique', *Antipode* 35(3): 415–42.

Nettles, K. D. (2007) 'Becoming Red Thread women: alternative visions of gendered politics in post-independence Guyana', *Social Movement Studies* 6(1): 57–82.

Peake, L. (1993) 'The development and role of women's political organizations in Guyana', in J. Momsen (ed.) *Women and Change in the Caribbean*, London: James Currey.

Red Thread (2005) *Organizing for Survival: Grassroots Women of the Flood*, DVD and transcript.

Red Thread (2006) 'Summary of experiences, lessons learned and recommendations.' Livelihoods paper presented by Andaiye, on behalf of women from the flooded communities organizing with Red Thread, at the Guyana Citizens' Initiative Seminar, 17 January.

Reddock, R. (1998) 'Women's organizations and movements in the Commonwealth Caribbean: the response to global economic crisis in the 1980s', *Feminist Review* 59: 57–73.

Rodney, W. (1981) *A History of the Guyanese Working People 1881–1905*, Baltimore: Johns Hopkins University Press.

Rodney, W. (1982) *In Defence of Arnold Rampersaud*, Guyana: Working People's Alliance.

Roopnaraine, R. (2009) Personal correspondence, 24 March.

Trotz, D. A. (2004) 'Between despair and hope: towards an analysis of women and violence in contemporary Guyana', *Small Axe: A Journal of Criticism* 15: 1–25.

Trotz, D. A. (2007) 'Red Thread in Guyana: the politics of hope', *Race and Class* 49(2): 71–8.

Westmaas, N. (2005) 'Mother of all floods: floods in Guyana's history' *Guyana Review*.

GUADELOUPE IS OURS

The Prefigurative Politics of the Mass Strike in the French Antilles

Yarimar Bonilla

University of Virginia, USA

In the early months of 2009, the French Caribbean island of Guadeloupe witnessed the largest wave of social protest in its history. A coalition of 48 different syndical, cultural, political, and civic organizations came together in order to protest against profiteering, exploitation and the 'expensive life' that characterizes life in the French Antilles. Armed with a list of 120 claims that spanned the terrain of disability rights, environmental policies, cultural nationalism, syndical freedom and increased wages, these Guadeloupean militants took to the streets, unified in their assertion that 'Guadeloupe is ours, not theirs'. Through their movement they effectively asserted their right to shape the course of their social, economic and political futures – despite their ongoing colonial relationship with France. In this essay I explore the impact of this strike on the Guadeloupean political imagination and examine the glimpses it provides into the current political climate, and future political horizon, of the French Antilles.

In the early months of 2009, the French Caribbean island of Guadeloupe witnessed the largest wave of social protest in its history. For a period of forty four days the entire society was paralysed by a general strike: schools and universities were closed, all major commerce was suspended, banks shut down, government services were discontinued, restaurants were shuttered, hotel rooms emptied, public transportation came to a halt, barricades blocked major roadways, and petrol distribution was suspended throughout the entire island, forcing drivers to park their cars and become pedestrians for over a month and a half. In Guadeloupe (and the French Caribbean more generally) labour stoppages and lockouts are relatively common occurrences, and a favoured tool for the powerful labour unions in the region. However, the movement of 2009 was unique in that it was not simply a labour strike, but truly a society wide mass strike that impacted the general social fabric and political imagination of the French Antilles.

From January through March – a time usually characterized by carnival parades and the high season of tourism – the general strike took hold of the public imagination and transformed quotidian life. Rather than rushing off to school and work, Guadeloupeans found themselves at home, talking with their neighbours, and engaging in different social relationships and practices. With the large-scale supermarkets and department stores inaccessible, residents turned to local fishermen, small-scale farmers, impromptu fruit vendors, and their own 'creole' gardens to supplement their meals. They found themselves consuming more fruits and vegetables, realizing that they could live without the French imports they had grown accustomed to, and even without the clutter of fast-moving European cars that usually clog the island's tiny roadways. When even propane gas distribution came to a halt, some residents turned to previous cooking practices, relighting their long-extinguished wood and charcoal stoves and 'rediscovering' traditional culinary practices.

Every aspect of this social revolution was documented in both traditional media outlets (newspapers, magazines, television and radio) and the emerging forms of 'new media' that have become increasingly important in Guadeloupe (social networking sites, blogs and other forms of interactive social technology). Negotiations with local employers and state bureaucrats were transmitted live on all local TV stations, call-in radio shows were dominated by commentary on the strike, and a new spate of blogs and websites flourished – many in direct support of the strike. The large amount of media coverage in turn fuelled massive demonstrations of popular support. During the strike, Guadeloupeans took to the streets in unprecedented numbers. First, 20,000, then 40,000, then 60,000, then up to 1000,000 people (nearly a quarter of the island's population) participated in mass marches in support of the movement. Observers repeatedly exclaimed that this was *du jamais vu* – something never before seen (or even imagined) – and many former nationalist activists declared that they could now die in peace because they had finally witnessed 'the awakening' of the Guadeloupean people.

In this essay I explore the impact of this strike on the Guadeloupean political imagination and examine the glimpses it provides into the current political climate, and future political horizon, of the French Antilles. I argue that the strike generated a moment of political exploration through which new collective alternatives could be imagined, invoked and rehearsed. During this time Guadeloupeans experimented with alternative forms of community, authority and collectivity. The strike thus served as a pre-figurative moment in which alternative economic, social and political configurations could be both imagined and experienced.

The notion of a prefigurative politics – of a politics that anticipates and rehearses that which it seeks to create – has been said to be one of the defining characteristics of our contemporary social movements (Graeber 2002; Polletta 2002; Juris 2008). However, the idea of political praxis – of the intrinsic relationship between thought and action – pre-dates contemporary activism, and is in fact an important element of the 'old' class-based politics, of which the mass strike is in many ways emblematic. As Rosa Luxemburg suggests, the mass strike constitutes a complex historical and political *process* – which takes shape in relationship to the social landscape in which it is embedded. It is thus not a universal political tool or strategy, but rather a culturally and historically specific moment of political action and explora-tion. Luxemburg describes the labour strike as 'the phenomenal form' of the proletarian struggle, and argues that it is 'the living pulse-beat of the revolution and at the same time its most powerful driving wheel' (Luxemburg and Scott 2008: 141). In other words, she sees the strike not merely as the expression of a collective will, but rather as a potential site for developing and prefiguring political alternatives. During a strike a new politics can materialize – both ideologically and phenomenologically.

This is not to say that labour strikes are inherent moments of revolutionary transformation. In fact, it is no longer certain whether the modernist concept of revolution remains a salient political category for our times (Scott 1995). However, it is important to recognize that labour strikes can generate a conceptual clearing by providing a break from the nexus of quotidian life. Strikes involve a suspension of work, a renegotiation of time and space, an engagement in new social relationships with co-workers and family, and a momentary rupture with the wage economy. As Walter Benjamin (1978) suggests, they represent moments of violent suspension, of the questioning of norms, and the assertion of collective and legal subjects.

In what follows I explore how the strike of 2009 served as a moment of political rupture in Guadeloupe. I argue that militants and their supporters were able to experiment with new forms of collectivity and authority that allowed them to reimagine the Guadeloupean population as a legible political subject. I examine the strike as a particular historical and political process – embedded in both the global economic context of our times, as well as the particular postcolonial legacies of Guadeloupe. However, taking heed of the recent calls to reexamine the stories we tell about colonialism and its aftermaths (Wilder 2005; Mbembe 2001; Dubois 2004; Cooper 2005), I approach the strike as a postcolonial movement driven by neither the romance (Edmondson 1999) nor the tragedy (Scott 2004) of postcolonial nationalism. For, as we have seen, a focus on the tropes of colonial emancipation can inadvertently obscure non-normative moments of political negotiation, which are perhaps less romantic, less tragic, more pragmatic, but still imaginative, proleptic and uniquely utopian (Wilder 2009).

In the case of Guadeloupe, it is important to remember that even though its contemporary political actors are the inheritors of a previous era of anticolonial thought and struggle, they are also the product of a particular political project of decolonization through juridical integration. As such, they inhabit a privileged position from which to rethink the categories of nation, citizenship, sovereignty and authority – given that these concepts have never been successfully packaged into a (however tenuously) guaranteed bundle of rights and duties (c.f. Ong 2006; Sassen 2006). As a result, their political imagination is shaped by a cynical stance towards both the emancipatory narrative of independence (Scott 1999), as well as the high-modernist promise of economic development and social engineering emanating from the colonial state (Scott 1998). Decolonization in the French Caribbean has been characterized by political and ideological exceptionalism. It has been marked by unthinkable histories (Trouillot 1995), paradoxical citizenships (Dubois 2004; Wilder 2005) and untimely political imaginaries (Wilder 2009). In what follows, I explore the development of one such seemingly improbable project and attempt to parse out the political categories and collective possibilities it both invokes and conjures.

Pwofitasyon: A New mot d'ordre in the French Antilles

It is important to note that the strike of 2009 in Guadeloupe was carried out not by a single trade union, but by a broad coalition of forty eight different political, economic, cultural, and syndical organizations. This included a wide assortment of labour federations, political parties, former pro-independence militants and nationalist activists, as well as what could be described as Guadeloupe's civil society: environmental groups, consumer rights' associations, advocates for disability rights, fair housing proponents, and even several cultural associations – particularly those promoting local gwo ka music and dance. The forging of this coalition is a significant development in an area that has long been characterized by fractured movements and deep political rifts. In fact, many suggested that one of the biggest accomplishments of the 2009 movement was simply to be able to bring such a variety of actors together within a shared political agenda.

Initially, the movement centred on petrol prices, which in recent years had reached astronomical levels – purportedly higher than in all of Europe. However, as different organizations joined the effort, the agenda expanded to include a wide range of issues, including the rising cost of housing, public services, banking fees, public transportation, basic necessities (milk, eggs, bread, basic hygiene products, etc.) and the various aspects of what is often described as 'the expensive life' (*la vie chére*) in the French Antilles. It also tackled wider problems stemming from a lack of local governance and planning, such as the decline of the local fishing industry, the lack of support for local artistic and cultural ventures, failures in the educational system, the need for environmental planning, greater job opportunities, and professional training initiatives.[1] This wide range of claims was brought together under the banner of *pwofitasyon* – a creole concept that evokes both exploitation and profiteering – and eventually the collective itself became known as the *Lyannaj Kont Pwofitasyon* (LKP), which can be loosely translated as the Alliance against Profiteering.[2]

In many ways this alliance resembles the kind of 'network politics' that are said to typify contemporary social movements (particularly international anti-corporate globalization movements). This new form of political action, which came to national attention after the 1999 anti-WTO protests in Seattle, is known for its ability to rally a wide range of political actors and agendas (agricultural workers, labour unions, environmentalists, etc.) against a common enemy (global corporate capitalism and its regulatory institutions) and for its decentralized forms of organization and consensus-based decision-making (Juris 2008; Graeber 2002). Many argue that this new form of network activism differs sharply from previous forms of labour politics. For example, Jeffrey Juris suggests that the 'command-oriented logic' of traditional labour parties and unions (with their vertical structures and focus on political consolidation) stands in sharp contrast to new forms of network-based politics focused around 'the creation of broad umbrella spaces, where diverse organizations, collectives, and networks converge around a few common hallmarks, while preserving their autonomy and identity based specificity' (Juris 2008: 14).

At first glance, the LKP coalition might seem like a clear example of this new form of coalition politics. In fact, there are numerous echoes of the anti-corporate globalization movement present in both the political content and organizational form of the LKP. However, it is important to note that although the LKP was able to assemble a wide diversity of political actors, it was still mostly dominated by labour organizations. As one militant explained, the labour unions served as the *moteur* of the organization:

1 The complete platform is available at www.lkp-gwa.org/revendications.htm and has also been published (symbolically enough) in the form of a little red book (see LKP 2009)

2 It is important to note that the LKP quickly inspired the development of similar movements throughout the French overseas departments. In Martinique activists came together as the Collectif du 5 fevrier (C5F), in Réunion activists launched a strike under the name COPSAR (Collectif des Organisations Syndicales, Politiques, et Associatives de la Réunion), and in Guyana activists forged a new collective named Mayouri Kont Lesplatasyon (MKL) in direct allusion to the LKP. Each of these movements took shape in response to the particular social and political context in which they were embedded; they were in contact with each other, but did not strategize or negotiate collectively.

providing both the driving force and the navigational steering for the movement. The development of the LKP should thus not be seen as a shift away from labour organizing, but rather as an expansion of the labour movement beyond the realm of shop floor politics.[3] The LKP is culmination of a powerful, dynamic and wide-reaching labour movement that emerged in Guadeloupe (and the former French colonies more generally) in the wake of an embattled anticolonial movement.

In some ways the emergence of the LKP can been seen as a response to the effects of a larger 'global economic crisis' characterized by the decline of local economic markets, dependence on foreign imports, the increased cost of staple goods, stunted national economic development, unregulated banking practices, the deskilling of labour, and the depressed wages allocated to workers throughout the world.[4] However, at the same time, the demands they formulated were also deeply rooted in the particular history of economic exploitation and racial inequality that characterizes the French Antilles. As Christine Chivallon (2009) notes, the political concept that emerged in Guadeloupe, *pwofitasyon*, semantically unites exploitation and profit, in a way that foregrounds the fundamental relationship between the search for wealth and the issue of its unfair allocation. There is no single term in English (or French) that can singlehandedly capture this creole concept, which is rooted in the deep colonial history of Caribbean societies.

It should be noted that as a French overseas department, Guadeloupe affords relatively high salaries and standards of living compared with other Caribbean societies. It has one of the highest per capita incomes in the region, and the minimum wage is the same as in France (almost $1,200 per month when the strike began). However, these high salaries are accompanied by even higher prices on most consumer goods and services – ranging anywhere from 20 to 170 per cent more expensive than in mainland France. Merchants argue that high transportation costs, taxes and tariffs oblige them to charge more for imported goods. Local political activists contend that the high prices are also the product of a larger racial and economic history.

The fact is, the economy in Guadeloupe has long been controlled by a small white minority, commonly referred to as the *békés*, that dominates the majority of the import-export industry and most major wholesale and retail operations. These elites are seen as the direct descendants, in both biological and economic terms, of the area's previous generations of plantation owners and slaveholders. It was partly the fear that independence from France would consolidate the *békés*' economic dominance that led many in the region, including intellectuals like Aimé Cesaire, to turn to the political project of French incorporation as a possible escape from the economic dominance of the planter class. In the face of an exploitative and racially self-segregating economic elite, the politicians of Cesaire's generation embraced the promises of political and economic equality represented by the French

3 As Linden Lewis (2009) suggests, this kind of political alchemy is precisely what is needed for the revitalization of Caribbean labour movements in the current era of global capital.

4 It is interesting to note that food riots against *la vie chère* had exploded in Haiti just one year prior to the Guadeloupe movement.

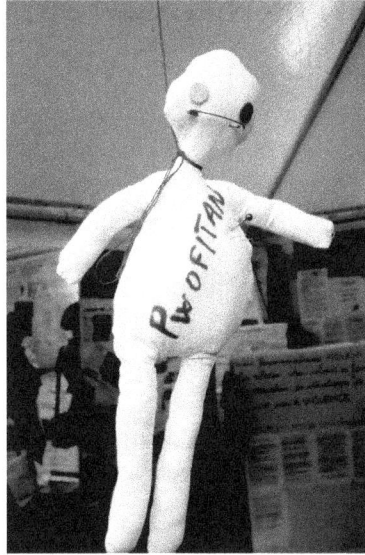

Figure 1 Effigy of a white *béké pwofitan* (photo by author)

Republic (Burton 1978; Constant 1998). As Justin Daniel suggests, 'obtaining rights from the state was the path followed by these classes to take revenge on history and to struggle against the *békés* (white creole class) and their hegemony' (2001: 64).

However, the project of political integration quickly proved disappointing in the Antilles. After Guadeloupe's integration into the French Republic in 1946, the local economy collapsed, unemployment skyrocketed, residents left in massive numbers for mainland France in search of employment opportunities, and dependence on the French state deepened – while the economic dominance of the *béké* class only increased. These economic elites have proven to be surprisingly resilient, quickly adapting to global economic tides and changing economic patterns in the Caribbean. They were able to shift from a production-based plantation model to a consumption-driven, import, tourist, and service dominated economy. As a result, the *békés* continue to be synonymous with the 'owning class' – they have successfully morphed from planters into businessmen by continuing to control the shifting means of production in the French Antilles (Vogt 2005: 254). Meanwhile, the popular classes in Guadeloupe are faced with significant economic and social challenges: with an unemployment rate of 25 per cent, compared with France's 8.1 per cent, and twice the French poverty rate (12.5 per cent versus 6.5 per cent), the contemporary economic landscape seems bleak, particularly for local youth (the unemployment rate is currently 55.7 per cent for those under 25).

Sé Tan Nou: Deciphering the Political Project of the LKP

The members of the LKP assert that they are united in their critique of the contemporary Guadeloupean social and economic landscape, but that they do not have a common political vision for the future. Although they offered a concept with which to describe their target of reform – *pwofitasyon* – they did not offer a parallel concept for the politic initiatives they sought to implement. Some of the organizations in the collective are known for their pro-independence ideology, but others do not share it; in fact, many of the members claim to have no political leanings at all, save for their opposition to high prices. However, as several prominent Antillean intellectuals have argued, the seemingly 'prosaic' search for greater purchasing power carries with it a broader 'poetic' gesture (Breleur et al. 2009) which has been interpreted as a desire for more local sovereignty and autonomy, if not necessarily outright independence. The LKP itself never issued a call for independence or sovereignty. However, during the course of the strike, a popular chant emerged as the quasi-official slogan of the movement:

La Gwadloup sé tan nou	Guadeloupe, it is ours
La Gwadloup sé pa ta yo	Guadeloupe, it is not theirs
Yo pé ké fè sa yo vlé adan péyi	They cannot do as they
an nou!	please in our country![5]

5 I am following here Jean Bernabé's (2009) proposed interperation of the creole term *sé* as 'it is' rather than simply 'is'. He argues that this better represents Guadeloupean creole usage, and that it more properly captures the gesture of self-affirmation that the song represents.

6 The song is widely available on the Internet, including at www.caribcreole1.com/news/guadeloupe/1,1000,20-02-2009-la-gwadloup-se-tan-nou.html.

The song – written by Jacky Richard, a local bank worker and LKP supporter, who said that the words had come to him in a dream – soon became the preferred political chant at rallies and demonstrations and was eventually recorded and released as a single by the groups Akyo and Vokum.[6] During the strike, these lyrics seemed to echo out of every corner in Guadeloupe: they were shouted by thousands of demonstrators during mass rallies, sung by children on the playground, blasted out of car radios and open windows, and emblazoned upon thousands of T-shirts sold by informal vendors on the side of the road.

The slogan's ambiguity might explain its popularity, for it is unclear what exactly is being claimed or asserted in this moment of enunciation. Some have suggested that the phrase represents a simple claim to territorial ownership (Giraud 2009: 77), while others have argued that it constitutes a deeper form of self-affirmation (Bernabé 2009). The fact is that the song constitutes a complex semiotic vehicle, carrying with it multiple layers of information. The communicative power of the slogan lies partly in the indexical function of the terms 'us' and 'them' (Jakobson 1971; Silverstein 1976). As linguistic shifters, these terms both presuppose and call into being the very social categories that frame their usage (Silverstein 1976: 53). They crystallize the social relationships that they reference by simultaneously

Figure 2 Massive demonstration organized by the LKP in Pointe-a-Pitre (photo by Dominique Chomereau-Lamotte)

hailing and naturalizing the categories they invoke. The fact that protestors could march down the streets invoking an abstract 'us' and 'them' (and be broadly understood) presupposes a shared social understanding of who and what those categories represent. It was not the existence of an 'us' and 'them' that caused controversy, but rather the claims being made about the proper place of those groups in the Guadeloupean hierarchy. In other words, it was not simply a matter of who belonged in these categories, but of the broader implications of that belonging.

As has been suggested, the demands of the LKP do not easily fit into the traditional debates over cultural identity and political status in the French Antilles (Giraud 2009: 74). Even though many of its main leaders were known to be advocates of independence, they refused to embed the movement in a pro-independence agenda. In fact it was the French president, Nicolas Sarkozy, who placed the strike within a discussion of greater political autonomy – an offer that was quickly embraced by local elected politicians, but not by the LKP. For the LKP leadership, the French government's initiative offered no real avenues for social transformation. They argue that this project did not spring out of the needs and desires of the Guadeloupean people, but was instead part of the wider efforts of the French government to decentralize and dismantle its welfare state system. In their eyes, the presumptive move towards greater 'local responsibility' was a simple transfer of administrative duties, without the economic and political means to carry

Figure 3 Protestors confront French Gendarmes at a barricade in Petit-Bourg (photo by Dominique Chomereau-Lamotte)

out true self-determination. They argue that they are not interested in administering the current political system, but in radically transforming it.

The LKP movement thus indexes the exhaustion of current political models in Guadeloupe, where both political incorporation and political independence have lost their promise and have become what can be described as 'futures past' (Koselleck 1985; Scott 2004). This movement emerges out of a desire for new political projects and formulas. It does not represent a new political doctrine, but an attempt at political improvisation and the rehearsal of collective formulas that have yet to take on concrete form. As Raymond Gama, one of the spokespersons for the LKP, explains:

> People like us are in the process of inventing new relationships ... we are in the process of saying for example that we can be in the UN without being French, and without necessarily having a Guadeloupean state. It's a bit of a paradox, but we are trying to create a new concept of political organization. Maybe we will find it within the French collectivity – not being French while at the same time being in the French ensemble ... I don't know ... . What I do know is that we are creating something that has already been promised, but which no one can imagine except us. We feel it, we live it, but we don't have the concepts with which to delimit it.

As Gama's words suggest, this new political project is in the process of its own conceptualization; it is yet to be imagined, yet to be constructed, and exists only as a possibility. The 2009 strike was thus not the manifestation of this new political subject but its prefiguration. As Gama suggests, it is during this time that a new form of community is 'lived' and 'felt' even before it can be articulated. The mass strike served as a moment of experimentation, through which activists were able to imagine, construct and inhabit (even if only temporarily) a new social and political collective. In fact, one Internet commentator suggested that the ambiguous *nou* invoked in the LKP song was nothing other than the manifestation of this collective spirit, the effervescence and fervour of the crowd marching and chanting in unison. It represents a figure that is both actual and imagined, emergent but unguaranteed. As Gama suggests, it has only been promised; it has been glimpsed, but never fully seen.

Conclusion

At a time when political leaders throughout the world were heralding the arrival of an epic economic crisis and an allegedly unforeseeable financial apocalypse, Guadeloupean activists dared to spark a massive political and economic upheaval that brazenly ignored global calls for economic and fiscal restraint. In the process, they shed new light, not only on the current economic landscape, but also on the deeper economic, racial and colonial legacies that have underpinned the global economic infrastructure of our age. In addition, they provided a glimpse, however fleeting, of an alternative political subject – a new Guadeloupean collective spirit that responded not to the political categories of revolutionary or nationalist political scripts, but to a uniquely pragmatic and strategically utopian quest for economic and political self-determination, unconstrained by the traditional constraints and boundaries of postcolonial politics in the Caribbean.

In the end, the strike of 2009 can generally be considered fruitful: LKP leaders reached an agreement with the government on 120 different points of reform, including a 200 euro monthly salary increase for minimum-wage workers, fixed prices on basic food items, reduced public transportation costs, rent control for public housing, and a review of public utility rates (among other gains). After forty four days of social paralysis the strike was lifted: schools, petrol stations and businesses reopened and Guadeloupeans slowly returned to their quotidian routines of life and work. However, it is impossible to say what the true outcome of the strike will be. At this point, negotiations with employers still continue, many of the concessions that were won have proved difficult to implement, demonstrators face significant legal charges, food prices have been lowered on some items but they have spiked on others, and promised development projects have yet to materialize. LKP leaders assert that the strike has been 'suspended' rather than completed, and in fact the new slogans on the T-shirts and banners in Guadeloupe do not proclaim victory, but offer instead yet another ambiguous slogan: 'nothing will ever be like it was before' (*ayen pé ké kon avan*). Many residents assert that the strike transformed the political and social fabric of their society. They argue that after a month and a half of disengagement from the consumer economy and of re-engagement with their family and neighbours, they will never be the same. As David Graeber suggests, 'It's one thing to say, "Another world is possible". It's another to experience it, however momentarily' (2002: 73).

Whether or not the political opening created by the LKP flourishes, its significance as a historical act is undeniable. As Gary Wilder (2009) has shown, even political alternatives that are foreclosed can still serve as important political legacies for the future. In fact, he suggests that herein lies the power of strategic utopianism: by acting as if the future was already here one can awaken imminent possibilities in the present (Wilder 2009: 105). Thus, rather than focusing on the revolutionary politics of a 'future past', the strike in Guadeloupe encourages us to explore the new futures of our present – those new political alternatives that become possible at the very moment in which they are prefigured.

References

Benjamin, W. (1978) 'Critique of violence', in *Reflections: Essays, Aphorisms, Autobiographical Writing* P. Demetz (ed.), New York: Harcourt Brace.

Bernabé, J. (2009) 'Gwadloup sé tan nou, mais qui est ce "Nou"?' *Carib Creole One*, online at www.caribcreole1.com/news/martinique/1,1106,18–03–2009-gwadloup-se-tan-nou-mais-qui-est-ce-nou-.html.

Breleur, E., Chamoiseau, P., Domi, S., Delver, G., Glissant, E., Pigeard de Gurbert, G., Portecop, O., Pulvar, O. and William, J.-C. (2009) *Manifeste pour les 'produits' de haute nécessité*. Paris: Galaade.

Burton, R. D. E. (1978) *Assimilation or Independence? Prospects for Martinique*. Occasional monograph series, Centre for Developing-Area Studies, McGill University No. 13. Montreal: Centre for Developing-Area Studies, McGill University.

Chivallon, C. (2009) 'Guadeloupe et Martinique en lutte contre la 'profitation': du caractère nouveau d'une histoire ancienne', *justice spatiale | spatial justice* 1, online at www.jssj.org/06.php.

Constant, F. (1998) 'French republicanism under challenge: white minority (*Béké*) power in Martinique and Guadeloupe', in H. Johnson and K. S. Watson (eds) *The White Minority in the Caribbean*, Kingston: Ian Randle Press.

Cooper, F. (2005) *Colonialism in Question: Theory, Knowledge, History*, Berkeley: University of California Press.

Daniel, J. (2001) 'The construction of dependency: economy and politics in the French Antilles', in R. A. Gamaliel and R. A. Israel (eds) *Islands at the Crossroads: Politics in the Non-Independent Caribbean*, Kingston: Ian Randle Press.

Dubois, L. (2004) *A Colony of Citizens: Revolution and Slave Emancipation in the French Caribbean, 1787–1804*, Chapel Hill: University of North Carolina Press.

Edmondson, B. (1999) *Caribbean Romances: The Politics of Regional Representation*, Charlottesville: University Press of Virginia.

Giraud, M. (2009) 'Les crises antillaises et le double fond de l'identité', in L. Laventure and F. Durpaire (eds) *La Révolution antillaise: quelle place pour l'outre-mer dans la république?*, Paris: Eyrolles.

Graeber, D. (2002) 'The new anarchists', *New Left Review* 13: 61–73.

Jakobson, R. (1971) 'Shifters, verbal categories and the Russian verb', in *Selected Writings of Roman Jakobson*, Vol. 2, The Hague: Mouton.

Juris, J. S. (2008) *Networking Futures: The Movements against Corporate Globalization*, Durham, NC: Duke University Press.

Koselleck, R. (1985) *Futures Past: On the Semantics of Historical Time, Studies in Contemporary German Social Thought*, Cambridge, MA: MIT Press.

Lewis, L. (2009) 'The alchemy of capital: Caribbean labour in the post-Cold War era.' Paper presented at the 34th Annual Conference of the Caribbean Studies Association, Kingston, Jamaica, 1–5 June.

LKP (2009) *Guadeloupe et martinique en grève générale contre la vie chère et l'exploitation outrancière: les 120 propositions du collectif*, Fort-de-France: Desnel.

Luxemburg, R. and Scott, H. (2008) *The Essential Rosa Luxemburg: Reform or Revolution and The Mass Strike*, Chicago: Haymarket Books.

Mbembe, A. (2001) *On the Postcolony*, Berkeley: University of California Press.

Ong, A. (2006) *Neoliberalism as Exception: Mutations in Citizenship and Sovereignty*, Durham, NC: Duke University Press.

Polletta, F. (2002) *Freedom is an Endless Meeting: Democracy in American Social Movements*, Chicago: University of Chicago Press.

Sassen, S. (2006) *Territory, Authority, Rights: From Medieval to Global Assemblages*, Princeton: Princeton University Press.

Scott, D. (1995) 'Revolution/theory/modernity: notes on the cognitive-political crisis of our time', *Social and Economic Studies* 44(2/3): 1–23.

Scott, D. (1999) *Refashioning Futures: Criticism after Postcoloniality*, Princeton: Princeton University Press.

Scott, D. (2004) *Conscripts of Modernity: The Tragedy of Colonial Enlightenment*, Durham, NC: Duke University Press.

Scott, J. C. (1998) *Seeing Like a State: How Certain Schemes to Improve the Human Condition Have Failed*, New Haven: Yale University Press.

Silverstein, M. (1976) 'Shifters, linguistic categories, and cultural description', in K. H. Basso and H. A. Selby (eds) *Meaning in Anthropology*, Albuquerque: University of New Mexico Press.

Trouillot, M.-R. (1995) *Silencing the Past: Power and the Production of History*, Boston: Beacon Press.

Vogt, E. (2005) 'Ghosts of the plantation: historical representations and cultural difference among Martinique's white elite' dissertation, Anthropology Department, University of Chicago.

Wilder, G. (1999) 'Practicing citizenship in imperial Paris', in J. L. Comaroff and J. Comaroff (eds) *Civil Society and the Political Imagination in Africa: Critical Perspectives*, Chicago: University of Chicago Press.

Wilder, G. (2005) *The French Imperial Nation-State: Negritude and Colonial Humanism between the Two World Wars*, Chicago: University of Chicago Press.

Wilder, G. (2009) 'Untimely vision: Aimé Césaire, decolonization, utopia', *Public Culture* 21(1): 101–40.

Legacies Through The Lens:
A Photo Essay by Kathy Sloane

Mothers Group member, St. Lucia, 1991

Analysis, St. Lucia, 1991

Rally: Opportunities for Women Dock Workers, Grenada, 1983

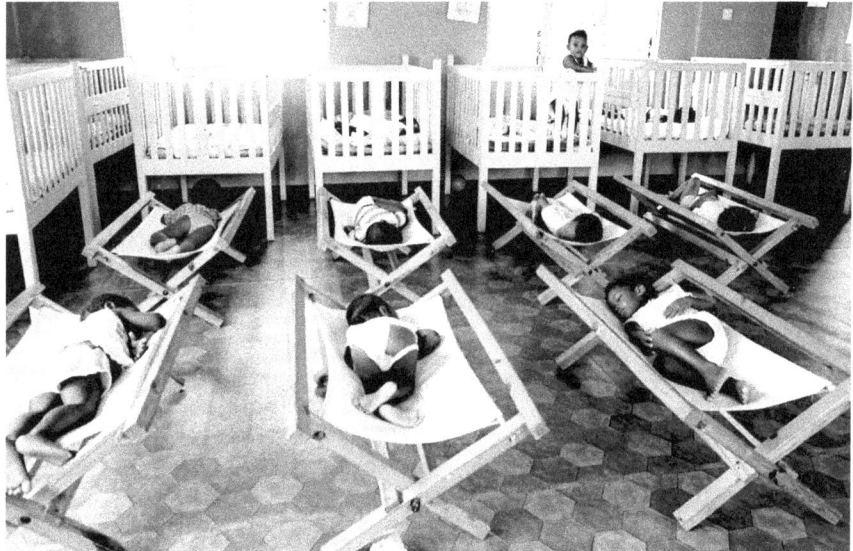

Legacy left: Laborie Day Care Center, Grenada, 1983

Index

Page numbers in **Bold** represent figures.

Routledge
Taylor & Francis Group

Journal of Literary Studies

Co-Published with UNISA Press

EDITORS:

Andries Oliphant, *University of South Africa*
Rory Ryan, *University of Johannesburg*

The *Journal of Literary Studies*, published in both English and Afrikaans, provides a forum for the discussion of literary theory, methodology, research, and related matters. It features articles, commentary, book reviews and general announcements. All contributions are peer-reviewed.

JOURNAL OF LITERARY STUDIES
TYDSKRIF VIR LITERATUURWETENSKAP

Volume 23 Number 1 March 2007

Recent Articles

The Postcolonial Gothic: Time and Death in Southern African Literature
Gerald Gaylard

Die problematiek van onthou: Die proses van herinnering in Antjie Krog se Country of My Skull
Ilse Groenewald

Imagery and Structure in Nadine Gordimer's "Once upon a Time"
Michael Shurgot

Story Skills and Hierarchies of Needs and Values: A Defence of the Humanities
Hein Viljoen

Athol Fugard's Exits and Entrances: The Playwright, the Actor and the Poet
Marisa Keuris

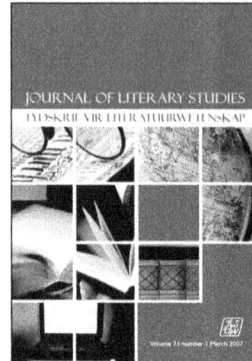

To sign up for tables of contents, new publications and citation alerting services visit **www.informaworld.com/alerting**

eupdates
Taylor & Francis Group

Register your email address at **www.tandf.co.uk/journals/eupdates.asp** to receive information on books, journals and other news within your areas of interest.

Powered by
informaworld

For further information, please contact Customer Services at either of the following:
T&F Informa UK Ltd, Sheepen Place, Colchester, Essex, CO3 3LP, UK
Tel: +44 (0) 20 7017 5544 Fax: 44 (0) 20 7017 5198
Email: subscriptions@tandf.co.uk Website: www.tandf.co.uk/journals

Taylor & Francis Inc, 325 Chestnut Street, Philadelphia, PA 19106, USA
Tel: +1 800 354 1420 (toll-free calls from within the US)
or +1 215 625 8900 (calls from overseas) Fax: +1 215 625 2940
Email: info@taylorandfrancis.com Website: www.taylorandfrancis.com
When ordering, please quote: XB90102A

View an online sample issue at:
www.tandf.co.uk/journals/rjls

For Product Safety Concerns and Information please contact our EU
representative GPSR@taylorandfrancis.com
Taylor & Francis Verlag GmbH, Kaufingerstraße 24, 80331 München, Germany